CONTENTS

**The main Sunday Service when the Lord's Supper is
not celebrated.**

APPROACH TO GOD

Call to worship

Praise

Call to prayer: (in words of holy scripture)

Prayers: Adoration
           Confession
           Absolution
           Supplication
           (Collect for the Day)

Praise

THE WORD OF GOD: HIS MIGHTY ACTS

*(A prayer for illumination or the Collect for the Day
may be said in association with the Readings or the
Sermon. The Readings may be separated by Praise,
traditionally from the Psalms.)*

Scripture Readings: Old Testament
                      New Testament—Epistle
                      New Testament—Gospel
                      (The Apostles' Creed)

B. ABELEDO

PRAYERS FOR SUNDAY SERVICES

PRAYERS FOR
SUNDAY SERVICES

Companion Volume to
The Book of Common Order (1979)

THE SAINT ANDREW PRESS
EDINBURGH

© The General Assembly's Panel on Worship 1980

First published 1980 by
THE SAINT ANDREW PRESS
121 George Street, Edinburgh
on behalf of
The General Assembly's
Panel on Worship

ISBN 0 86153 088 8

Reprinted 1986

Printed in Great Britain by
McCorquodale (Scotland) Ltd.

Praise

The Sermon: concluded with an Ascription of Praise.

RESPONSE TO THE WORD OF GOD

Praise (The Apostles' Creed)	*Praise* (The Apostles' Creed)
Prayers:	The Offerings

Intercession
    Commemoration
    of the Faithful
    Departed
	Prayers:

The Offerings	Thanksgiving
	    Self-dedication
	    Intercession
	    Commemoration
	    of the Faithful
	    Departed
	    The Lord's
	    Prayer

Prayers:	

Thanksgiving
    Self-dedication
    The Lord's
    Prayer	

Praise	*Praise*

DISMISSAL AND BENEDICTION

INTRODUCTION

This book contains sixteen full sets of prayers for Sundays when there is no celebration of Holy Communion; also prayers for different seasons of the Christian Year, and material for occasions when church furnishings are to be dedicated. It is intended to be used as a companion to *The Book of Common Order (1979)*.

The sets of prayers

All of these follow the order of worship outlined on pages 42–43 of *The Book of Common Order (1979)*, and reproduced here on pages vi and vii. The Committee on Public Worship and Aids to Devotion has departed from its previous practice of editing and standardising prayers, believing that there is no longer any one language of public prayer familiar and acceptable to the whole Church. These services therefore have been reproduced almost wholly as they were submitted, and they reflect the style and idiom of their different contributors. No new translation of the scriptures has risen to a position of such dominant influence on the language of worship as the Authorised Version enjoyed in the past, and a collection of prayers that is to be of value to the whole Church must echo something of the diversity now to be found within the Church. Leaders of worship must be prepared to select that material which they can use unselfconsciously in their own situation.

No separate provision has been made for evening services. This is not because the Committee believes that worship should be confined to one service each Sunday, but because the response to previously published orders for evening worship suggests that there is very little demand for new material.

Prayers for seasons of the Christian Year

The material included in this section is not a revision of the services in the 1952 edition of *Prayers for the Christian Year*. The provision of full services for every season suggests that each part of a service must somehow be related to its point in the calendar. The Committee believes it will be more helpful for leaders to have resource material, which can be slotted in to the framework of a service, than to have whole services constructed round seasonal themes. The types of prayer vary, so they will not all fit appropriately into the same part of a service.

Since there were no proper prefaces for the third Communion order in *The Book of Common Order (1979)*, three extended prefaces for the great seasons of the Christian Year have been included here. These reflect the Committee's conviction that modernity ought not to imply the jettisoning of all doctrinal or biblical substance in worship.

The Committee is well aware that this volume will not blaze any trails in the Church's worship. That is not its function. That function is rather to provide a quarry from which materials may be drawn by those who wish their services to stand in the main stream of the Church's tradition of worship.

DAVID M. BECKETT
January 1980   *Convener*

Prayers for Sixteen Services

SERVICE ONE

Sentences

The Lord lives, blessed is my rock,
high above all is God who saves me.

He set my feet on a rock
and gave me a firm footing;
and on my lips he put a new song,
a song of praise to our God.

Happy is the man who makes the Lord his trust.

Adoration

Father, whose love is working through all creation;
Son of God, in whose likeness we shall be made new;
Holy Spirit, touching our lives with hope:
Receive our worship; reclaim us for your service;
set us free to honour you today.

Glory be to God.

Confession and Absolution

Father eternal, giver of light and grace,
we have sinned against you and against our fellow
    men,
in what we have thought,
in what we have said and done,
through ignorance, through weakness, through our
    own deliberate fault.
We have wounded your love, and marred your image
    in us.
We are sorry and ashamed, and repent of all our sins.

3

For the sake of your Son, Jesus Christ, who died for us, forgive us all that is past,
and lead us out from darkness to walk as children of light.

A Silence

Minister:

"We have one to plead our cause with the Father, Jesus Christ, and he is just. He is himself the remedy for the defilement of our sins, not our sins only but the sins of all the world."
Your sins are forgiven, since you bear his name.

Supplication

Most gracious God, as you have affirmed our place among believers, strengthen us and all your people by the ever-present witness of your Spirit; that we may honour Christ in our words and in our deeds, to the glory of your holy name.

God and Father of our Lord Jesus Christ, from whom alone comes everlasting joy and peace; fill our hearts with joy in your promises of salvation, and send us as peacemakers and witnesses to your promises; through your Son Jesus Christ our Lord.

Thanksgiving

Most glorious Lord of life, we praise you for every encouragement you have given us in the service of Christ our Saviour:

for our homes, our families and our friendships in the faith;

for our work and for all opportunities of kindness;
for quickness of mind and body;
but most of all we bless you for your Son,
whose obedience to your will calls for our obedience,
whose suffering at the hands of sinners has brought
   forgiveness to us all,
who ever lives, and is our life, .
who will come again.

> Holy, holy, holy Lord,
> God of power and might,
> Heaven and earth are full of your glory,
> Hosanna in the highest.
> Blessed is he who comes in the name of the
>   Lord.
> Hosanna in the highest.

Self-Dedication and Intercession

Father, in Jesus' name accept and bless us and what
we offer for Christian witness to your love;
and mercifully hear us as now we pray:

for seasonable weather for farmers and gardeners;

for a smooth flow of materials to industry;

for good labour relations;

for young and old, as they rely on the earnings and
caring concern of others;

for all who are ill;

for the bereaved;

and for the under-privileged millions throughout the
world, whose poverty of living we can scarcely imagine
or understand.

Spirit of Love,
Fire your people with Christ's love for all mankind.
Come, Holy Spirit, come.

Commemoration

And now, Father, bring to our remembrance the unity of the church in heaven and on earth, fill us with the joy of the saints, and keep us faithful to you all the days of our service here on earth; through Jesus Christ our Lord,

in whose words we pray, and say, Our Father . . .

SERVICE TWO

Sentences

The Lord is in his holy temple, the Lord's throne is
  in heaven.
His eye is upon mankind, he takes their measure at a
  glance.

Adoration

Glory be to the Father and to the Son and to the Holy
  Spirit:
and upon us, weak and sinful, be mercy and grace at
  all times.

Father, you are waiting to bless the peoples of the
  world.
You are all-wise, alert to every need.

Jesus, you take your stand for sinners.
Bearer of mercy, you are mighty to save.

Holy Spirit, maker and re-maker of life,
You are all-patient, knowing the ways of God.

Confession and Absolution

In God's most holy presence, we acknowledge our
place in a world that is weary of its pain:

In mercy, O God, grant us sorrow over the sin in
  our life.

We have done wrong, and failed to do good.
We have followed our own hearts' desires.
Our spirits cry out for the right we see in our Lord.

Come down, O Love Divine.

A Silence

Minister:

Jesus died and rose again for you.

In humble penitence, take your pardon, know his peace.

Supplication

Father, as you have given us new life in Christ, give us grace to keep your commandments:

Live as servants of God; honour all men; love the brotherhood.

Do not nurse anger against your brother; overcome evil with good.

Know that your body is a temple of the Holy Spirit.

Lord our God, the battle of good and evil rages within and without, and our ancient foe tempts us with his deceits and empty promises.

Keep us steadfast in your Word; and when we fall raise us again and restore us, through your Son Jesus Christ our Lord.

Thanksgiving and Self-Dedication

Most loving Lord of life, we thank you for the air we breathe, for refreshing rain, for the warmth of summer sun.

We thank you that in our need of these things we are one with the earth—

the trees, the fields and all of nature.

But even as we thank you for all that makes our bodies strong, we thank you more for the upward call into life with Jesus Christ, life begun within time but which will last for ever, resurrection life.

We praise you for the ministry of word and sacraments, for the energies of the Holy Spirit—in the church and in the world—
preparing us for your glory.
Accept us in our worship and in our giving of ourselves into Christ's service;
for your mercy's sake.

Intercession

In our prayers for others, we pray to God in Jesus' name:

first of all for countries whose land is scarred by war and for people intimidated through violence done to those they love.

> Father, let your strong peace be sufficient to hold us in your will.

We commend to God our towns and cities, and everyone in our community here.
Where there is growth in understanding, may we gladly give thanks; where grudges are held, may they be cleared away.
In our prayers for the sick, we uplift to God people weak and damaged in body or in mind, some of them serene in spirit but others distressed.

> Father, meet with them in their present infirmity, and for the future give them hope.

We pray for families:
> for parents and children,
>> husbands and wives,
>> brothers and sisters,
>>> and for all who are very conscious that they live alone.

God give peace to our households and freedom in faith.

Commemoration

God, grant us throughout our mortal life unity with those who have loved us in faith, and in due time a peaceful death; through Jesus Christ our Lord

in whose words we further pray, Our Father . . .

SERVICE THREE

Sentences

Turn from evil and do good, seek peace and pursue it.
The eyes of the Lord are upon the righteous, and
his ears are open to their cries.

Approach

Almighty God you listen when we pray:
we worship and adore you.
O God, so willing to be found by those who seek you:
we worship and adore you.
O God, ready to forgive, gracious and loving:
we worship and adore you.

Confession and Supplication

O God, Father of all men:
have mercy upon us.
O God the Son, Saviour of sinners:
have mercy upon us.
O God the Holy Spirit, living in each of us:
have mercy upon us.

From love of money and desire for possessions:
O Lord deliver us.
From envy of the rich and scorn of the poor:
O Lord deliver us.
From class-bitterness and colour prejudice:
O Lord deliver us.
From anger, impurity and pride:
O Lord deliver us.
From dishonesty and slackness:
O Lord deliver us.
From doubt and despair, and from fear of death:
O Lord deliver us.

Collect (for the day)

Thanksgiving

Loving Father we thank you with grateful hearts:

for the wonders of the universe and for the fruits of this world;

for the development of mankind, the gifts and talents given them and for the blessings of social order;

for the pleasures of art and music, literature and drama, for the discoveries of science and the principles of justice;

for human love, for the comfort of homes and the companionship of friends;

for the forgiveness of sins, for the good news of the gospel and for the guidance and prayers of the church.

Dedication

Lord God, you have given us more than we asked for and more than we deserve. May we show a like generosity in all that we do for you and our fellow men; through Jesus Christ our Lord.

Intercession

Heavenly Father, by whom all men are equally loved, grant us such love and concern for others that we may sincerely pray for them.

We pray that the church may faithfully proclaim the good news to the world and bring all nations to your light; that men may be obedient to your voice in the church and helped by word and sacrament.

We pray that your grace may be given to our Queen, our government and our country, making our land a home for peace and justice, freedom and truth.

We pray that brotherhood may spread among all men that the hungry may be fed and the naked clothed.

We pray for those who earn their daily bread in cities or in the country, in factory or shop, with hand or with brain.

We ask you to heal the sick, to comfort the broken-hearted, to befriend the lonely, to support the aged and to console the dying.

Eternal God we give you thanks for those who sought and found you, loved and served you. From our memory of them may we become more devoted to you and gain a firmer faith that nothing will separate us from your love in Jesus Christ to whom with you and the Holy Spirit be glory for ever, world without end.

Our Father . . .

SERVICE FOUR

Sentences

The steadfast love of the Lord is from everlasting to everlasting upon those who fear him, and his righteousness to children's children.
Bless the Lord, all his works, in all places of his dominion.
Bless the Lord, O my soul.

Adoration

Eternal and ever-blessed God, the same yesterday, today and for ever,
we rejoice in the order and goodness of your creation.
Let the light of your love shine into our hearts and bless our worship, transforming it from its imperfection to an offering acceptable to you.
Help us to see new glory in the things we take for granted and lead us to praise you with our whole being.
May your joy be in our hearts and your love in our fellowship; through Jesus Christ our Lord.

Confession

Almighty God we confess that we have sinned in thought, word and deed.
We confess the sins that no one knows and the sins that everyone knows:
the sins that burden us and the sins that no longer trouble us.

We confess our sins as a church:
that we have not loved one another as Christ loved us;
that we have not forgiven one another us we have
    been forgiven;

14

that we have not given ourselves in sacrifice and love
for the world as Christ gave himself for us.

Father, forgive us and enable us to live as you would
have us live; through Jesus Christ our Lord.

Collect (for the day)

Thanksgiving

Lord God, we thank you for the creation and preservation of the world;
for the rhythm of day and night;
for the changing seasons.
We praise you for memory, imagination and foresight.
We thank you for your infinite patience with the
waywardness of men;
you have neither wearied of us, nor allowed us to
destroy ourselves;
you have sent your Son to break down the barriers
between us;
and to restore the broken unity of human life.
For these and all your gifts we thank you in his name.

Intercession

Almighty God, we pray for the church in the world;
that it may share fully in the work of Jesus Christ,
revealing you to men and reconciling men to you;
that Christians may learn to love one another as you
have loved us so that the visible church may more
and more exhibit that unity which is your gift.
We pray for the Royal Family and for our country:
that none of our people may exploit others, none be
neglected or forgotten; that we may be swift to reward

service and recognise worth; and that all may work for our common life and welfare.

We remember those who are ill; that illness may not break their spirit; that through the healing skill you have given they may be made well; that those permanently handicapped may find the way to use and overcome their disability.

Father, we pray for those who suffer for faith and are tempted to turn back because the way is hard; help them and strengthen them, so that they may hold out to the end and by their loyal witness draw others to you.

Commemoration

Father, we thank you for all the people, great and humble, who have maintained the fabric of the world's life in the past and left us a great inheritance. We pray that we may be counted worthy to share with them the life of your kingdom; through Jesus Christ our Lord, to whom with you, Father, and the Holy Spirit, in the majesty of the undivided Trinity, be dominion and praise for ever.

SERVICE FIVE

Sentences

Make a joyful noise unto the Lord, all ye lands,
Enter his gates with thanksgiving, and his courts with
    praise.
For the Lord is good,
His steadfast love endures for ever,
And his faithfulness to all generations.

Adoration

Let us worship the greatness of God.

The universe in its immensity surrounds us,
By night the silence and the splendour of the stars,
By day, the light shining longer and more brightly,
The promise of spring that lifts our hearts and our
    hopes,
All these things speak to us of God.
But what is man, that God should care for us?
He has not left us lonely in this world,
He has given us human friends to care for us,
He has come to each of us saying, "My son, my
    daughter, I love you for ever".
He has brought us into the family of his well-beloved
    Son . . .

Father, what can we do but thank you?

Confession and Absolution

Let us confess our sins.

Father, you know every thought of our hearts,
Every word that we speak,
Every temptation that attacks us.
The sins and weaknesses of each of us are so different;
Hear us then as in silence we bring them to mind,
Confessing them to you . . .

Be assured, that if we confess our sins, he is faithful
  and just to forgive us.

Let us now pray for ourselves.

We pray to you, Lord Jesus,
All authority in heaven and earth has been given to
  you,
Help us to be wise and bold in bearing witness to you,
In standing up for what is just, and kind, and generous
  to others.
If any one of us here is in special trouble, grant to him
  some special sign,
Some assurance that you have not forgotten him.
Give us confidence to meet our problems,
Knowing that we do not face them alone.
In your name we present our prayer.

Thanksgiving

God our Father,
We thank you for the great gift of life,
For all our happy and worthwhile experiences,
For the wonderful beauty of the world,
For our homes, our families, and our work,
For our medical services, and the healing they have
  brought to men,
Including ourselves, both in mind and in body.
We thank you for Jesus Christ and his church,
For the light that shines on our past, our present and
  our future because of him.
We thank you for Jesus himself, the hope of all the
  ends of the earth,
And for his coming triumph over all his enemies.

Intercession

Lord, we pray to you for those who govern us:
May they be given insight and courage.
We pray for those in . . . who are faced with uncertainty
and unemployment:
May our church and our nation not forget them.
We remember the distressed people of . . .
We remember the needs of the exploited, the hungry
and the despairing throughout the world.
May men find new ways of bringing love and justice
wherever there is need.
Hear us as in silence we pray for any who have asked
for our prayers, or who are especially dear to us.
Bless all young people.
Guide them to wise use of their growing powers.
May nothing we say or do cause them to stumble.
Protect them and help us to defend them from cruel
and selfish exploitation.
May they and we discover together your purpose for
our world.

Bless the church, its ministers and its people:
Give them great encouragement in their work.
In your time, Father, bring all your people into a unity
of love and faith, so that the world may know that
Jesus Christ is Lord, to your own glory and the
blessing of all men.

Our Father . . .

SERVICE SIX

Sentence

The Spirit you have received is not a spirit of slavery
leading you back into a life of fear, but a Spirit that
makes us sons, enabling us to cry "Abba! Father!".

Approach

Father, on this day set apart in the week to remind
us that time and history are in your hands, we devote
ourselves for a fleeting moment to worship you.

To this church building, set apart as a symbol of your
lordship over space and all material things, we come
—dwellers in time and space—to confess that you
are God.

"Know that the Lord is God. It is he who made us
and we are his. We are his people and the sheep of
his pasture. Enter his gates with thanksgiving and his
courts with praise."

Jesus is our gateway into your presence, Father. We
come gladly and freely in his name. The Holy Spirit
will fill us with thanksgiving and put words of praise
on our lips. We ask his help now to make our worship
live.

Confession and Assurance of Forgiveness

Jesus, Lamb of God, have mercy on us. We make
confession in the Psalmist's words.

"I am ready to fall, and my pain is ever with me. I
confess my iniquity.

"I am sorry for my sin. Those who are my foes without cause are mighty, and many are those who hate
me wrongfully.

"Do not forsake me, O Lord! O my God be not far
from me! Make haste to help me, O Lord my
salvation!" *(Silence)*

Jesus said, "Where are your accusers? Nor do I condemn you. Go and sin no more".

Supplication

We praise you, Father, for the reassurance of the Gospel. Make us worthy of our acceptance in Christ. Help us at each word of forgiveness to step forward into a closer walk with you, our faith growing to knowledge of the Lord, our witness more confident.
So with a love that is strong and a peace that robs worry of its power, we may indeed be changed from one degree of glory to another until you are as close to us as breathing, and your perfect light has chased the last shadow from our lives.
Jesus, Redeemer of the world, give us your peace.
Praise and honour, glory and might to him who sits on the throne and to the Lamb for ever and ever.

Oblation

Almighty God, who in Jesus came in flesh to live among us, we yield our lives and our substance to him who is true man.
Consecrate these gifts that through them the actions of the incarnate Christ may be done in this world which he loves.
Consecrate our lives that through them the word of the incarnate Christ may be spoken to the lives of this world for whom he gave himself;
Through the same incarnate Christ now glorified.

Thanksgiving

Most gracious God you have been merciful and loving towards us throughout all our years.

We give thanks for the Lord who lived and died and lives now for us; for our baptism when we were caught up into the life of Christ; for the Holy Spirit's guiding as we grew and still grow into our true humanity; for the sure promise that your Kingdom hid from many eyes will come in its fullness.

We praise you for countless things of beauty, interest and love which fill our lives. Help us at all times to master selfishness in pleasure—to give praise to you in all things—to avoid the use of other people or the abuse of creation for our own ends.

We thank you, Lord, for family and friends and Christian fellowship. If we had no one you would still be there beside us, but you have placed us in a circle of love, interest and compassion. How great is your love for us if this is but a pale reflection. Grant, Lord, that in all our relationships we may in turn pour out the love which has been shown to us.

Intercession

Father, we commend to your care and inspiration the whole Church of Jesus Christ. Grant in our time that the Church, strong in his unity may speak with one voice to the needs of the world.

Bless our own congregation, increasing our service to you and our usefulness in the witness of the universal Church.

Lead all who lead among us.

We pray for the influence of your Holy Spirit in the troubled places of the world. May he speak to Christian leaders that they may see not only political solutions but the will and mind of Christ. May peace on earth be the peace of God.

We pray for those of other faiths—the Jew, the
Muslim, the Hindu, the Buddhist, the Sikh, that
through your Holy Spirit counsels of peace may be
heard, and that glory may be given to you when all
things are revealed.

We pray for all who are happy and for whom things
are going well that they may know the source of their
blessing.

We pray for all who are distressed. Comfort the sad,
be present with the sick and make your will known
to them. Invigorate those who are depressed by failure.
In mercy, Father, grant answer to those prayers which
we now offer to you in silence . . .

Commemoration

With reverence and affection, our Father, we remember
before you our kindred and friends whom you have
called home. Keep us in union with them in Christ
through the Spirit that in time we too may come into
your presence and be numbered with those who serve
you in the joy and brightness of the Kingdom.

These prayers we present in the name of Jesus Christ
our High Priest in whose own words our worship
continues:

Our Father . . .

SERVICE SEVEN

Sentences

O come, let us worship and bow down. Let us kneel before the Lord, our Maker.

Approach

Lord God, you nourish and sustain the world from day to day and wherever we go you are with us more fully than we dare presume.
We thank you for this hidden yet faithful presence.
Make us receptive and open to your Spirit
and speak to us your word of peace, through Jesus Christ your Son.

Confession

Merciful Father, you care for each of us and for our happiness and when we turn from you and hurt one another your heart is grieved.

For our lack of understanding and for the bitterness we often feel;

for our forgetfulness and neglect of others and for the suffering we cause;

for our failure to forgive;

we seek your pardon.

We thank you for the assurance you have given us in Jesus

that you accept us as we are

and are ready to forgive us.

Fulfil that promise for us now,

that we may be released from past failure

and may venture a new beginning through Jesus Christ.

Supplication

Living God, you have called us to be your people,
to be a sign of hope in this wide, uncertain world;
we pray that you will equip us for work in your service.
Renew us according to the example of Christ.
Let us grow like him and no longer repay evil with evil,
but make peace,
and live in truth today and every day of our lives.
Our prayer is in Jesus' name.

Thanksgiving

God, our Creator and our Father:
We thank you for the gift of life,
for homes and food and health,
for all the things we take for granted,
for everything that comes to us all the time from you
We thank you for the people around us,
for the kindness of friends and the love of family,
for the affection by which we are sustained.
We thank you for today,
for the present age in which we live,
for a world in which you have given us so much power
and have called us to be neighbours to one another.

Dedication

Lord God, accept these our gifts. May our giving be
a sign of our commitment to live in this world as
your people.
Help us to see the wide horizons of your love and
give us sympathy and imagination as we pray for
others.

Intercession

We pray, Lord, for those with whom we share life:
for our families and for the strengthening of family life.
We pray for mutual trust wherever people work
   together,
for understanding in wage negotiations and sym-
   pathetic provision for those who have no work to do.

In prayer we remember those who have no home of
   their own and those who are badly housed.
We pray for all who have come to this country from
   overseas, that they may be received with hospitality;
and for those who live alone, that they may not be
   forgotten.

We pray, Lord, for our many brothers and sisters in
   other lands who are under the shadow of poverty
   and hunger;
for all who have to live with injustice and for those
   who have been broken and disabled by war.
Grant that those who are called to leadership among
   the nations may never cease in their attempts to find
   peace;
and enable us to play our part in working for justice
   and righteousness.

Heavenly Father, we commend to you those whose
   sickness finds no cure;
those who carry burdens of sorrow or failure;
those who are permanently handicapped.
Bless all who devote themselves to caring for others,
And grant that none may feel themselves forsaken by
   you.

We pray for your Church in this and every land.

Grant that those who are called to live and proclaim
the Gospel may point to your coming kingdom and
may seek the unity and peace of all your people.

God of the living, we thank you for all who have
trusted in your grace and gone before us in the way
of faith.

In the strength of this fellowship bring us to fullness
of life from day to day and to all eternity.

And to you Father, Son and Holy Spirit be glory and
praise.

SERVICE EIGHT

Sentence

God is love; he who dwells in love is dwelling in God, and God in him.

Approach

O Lord God, you are love, love above all love.
Wherever love is born, you are the creator;
Wherever love continues, you dwell;
Wherever love rules, you reign.
Love is your being and your action—a consuming fire.
Lord, by your love awaken ours.
By love help us to worship the love that is boundless, endless, divine.

Confession and Absolution

Merciful God, we have seen that in Christ's way of love there lies the secret of all life and the hope of all men, but we have been satisfied with lesser love and narrower affections. Forgive us if we have passed one another without recognition or greeting; if we have withheld the kindly deed or let loose the word of anger; if we have laboured to win a point and have lost a friend; if we have harboured resentment and plotted revenge. Forgive us and make us ready to forgive.

> Lord, have mercy upon us.
> Christ, have mercy upon us.
> Lord, have mercy upon us.

Let us hear from Scripture the assurance of God's pardon:

"This is what love is: it is not that we have loved God, but that he loved us and sent his Son to be the means by which our sins are forgiven."

Petition

Let us pray that we may grow in love:

Lord God, you made man in your own image, and you love all whom you have made: teach us to discern that image in our fellow men, and to love them for Christ's sake. May we not despise any for whom Christ died, nor injure any in whom he lives, but have fixed within our hearts his law of self-giving love, so that we may begin to love in his way, in gratitude for his love to us. For his Name's sake we ask it.

Intercession

We pray you, Lord God, to fan the flame of love in our hearts to give warmth to the words of our lips and the thoughts of our minds as we pray for others.

We pray for all whose love has grown cold—in situations where marriages are under strain, where there are tensions between the generations. Help them all to live with one another in gentleness, understanding and good humour.

We pray for all in situations where bitterness and hatred exclude love—for lands where men of differing race or colour fail to see their human brotherhood, and for communities torn by civil strife—(especially for . . .); for those parts of the world where warfare rages or smoulders, that its futility as a way of solving problems may soon be seen. Teach all who fight the worth of peace and tolerance.

We pray for all who have the responsibility of governing our country, of managing our industries and leading the trade unions, and who find it difficult to see how love should be applied; for those concerned with the penal system as they seek to maintain the worth of the individual and the safety of the community; for those who negotiate wages and working conditions. Teach all our leaders to fight for justice and not for sectional interest.

We pray for your church, established on earth to be a community of love, and yet so often divided and disputing. Teach her anew the reconciling power of Christ, that by her life and witness she may advance his kingdom in the world.

We pray in silence for all for whom we feel particular concern at present . . .

Hear all our prayers, Lord God, for the sake of Jesus Christ our Lord, who lives and reigns with you, our Father, and the Holy Spirit, one God for evermore.

Thanksgiving

Lift up your hearts.
> We lift them up to the Lord.

Let us give thanks to the Lord our God.
> It is right to give him thanks and praise.

With glad obedience to your law of love we bring the tribute of our thanksgiving. We praise you that by your goodness all things were created, are sustained in being, and will be brought to their perfect fulfilment. We thank you for the wonder and beauty of this world of ours, for the gradually unfolding disclosure of its marvellous resources, and for our human race in its glory and its shame. We thank you for your saving purpose and redeeming power revealed in Christ, by which we are rescued from the sinful folly of our ways. All your works are acts of love, and in responding love we join with those who, in your nearer presence, sing the eternal song of loving adoration.

> Holy, holy, holy Lord, God of power and might,
> heaven and earth are full of your glory.
> Hosanna in the highest.

Oblation

Creator Spirit, without whose power no good was ever done, we believe it to be your will to make on earth one family of men, living together in love and joy and peace as citizens of heaven. Fulfil this holy purpose through us your servants. Take the labour of our hands and minds, our time, our talents, and possessions, and make of this rough-hewn humanity a perfect fellowship as promised in our Saviour Jesus Christ.

Remembrance

Keep us, O Lord, united in faith and hope and love with those dear to us who have entered into their rest, and with all the faithful departed; and bring us in the end to your eternal joy; through Jesus Christ our Lord, in whose words we further pray and say:

> Our Father . . .

(This service was made for use on the 7th Sunday after Pentecost following the Joint Liturgical Group Calendar and Lectionary (2nd year).)

SERVICE NINE

Sentence

Our mouths shall praise God with joy: our souls shall be filled as with a banquet, because the loving kindness of God is better than life.

Adoration

Glory be to God the Father, the creator of all things:
Glory be to God, the Son, the Redeemer:
Glory be to God the Holy Spirit, the sanctifier of the faithful:
To the one God and Holy Trinity be glory.

Confession and Absolution

Let us confess in God's presence that for too much of the time we are blind to God's glory and forgetful of his loving-kindness. We are casual about the colours of the autumn and the unspeakable marvel of the universe and insensitive to the vast range and sweep of the Father's providence and the gentleness of his love. We are blind to the glory of Christ's works and ways and we cannot believe they could redeem our times. We are blind to the glory of the Spirit's sanctifying power and will not believe that it can reverse the unholy trends or penetrate the complexities of our national situation, or sweeten the bitterness of political life.

O God forgive us our blindness and faithlessness through Jesus Christ our Lord.

Jesus once said to a man: Have back your sight; your faith has made you whole.

Supplication

O God, you have made us heirs of all the victories of faith, and joint heirs with Christ of your glory, if we suffer with him: arm us with such trust in the truth that is invisible, that we may ask no rest from its demands and have no fear in its service; through Jesus Christ our Lord.

Thanksgiving

We bless you and praise you, O God. We rejoice in our most holy faith that as God the Father, you love the children of men, that in the midst of time and here upon the earth you have planted a kingdom that is not overthrown by time nor limited by earth's finitude. We bless you for Jesus Christ, the architect and maker of that kingdom and the giver of its holy laws of love. We praise you for the Holy Spirit instructing us in the ways of that kingdom and inspiring us to pursue with courage its holy ideals. Glory be to the Father, and to the Son, and to the Holy Spirit: as it was in the beginning, is now, and ever shall be, world without end.

We bless you for those who, guided by the Spirit, have sought to give expression to Christian values in the organisations of the church in our day, (for 80 years of Boys' Brigade in this place), for good traditions that have grown up, for fellowship, for precious memories.

Truly, O Lord, it is right that we should praise you and give thanks when we remember your goodness.

Intercession

Let us pray God, through Jesus Christ our Lord, to bless the church and all who serve in her, those who sow in tears, and those who neglect the harvest and those who return from mission rejoicing, bearing their sheaves with them.
Lord in your mercy,
    Hear our prayer.

Let us pray for peace on earth; let us recall the stinging accusation that has been made that men prepare for war like giants, and for peace like stunted pygmies, and let us pray God, through Jesus Christ our Lord, to bless all the peacemakers upon earth.
Lord in your mercy,
    Hear our prayer.

Let us pray God, through Jesus Christ our Lord, to bring industrial peace to this land, not least to Scotland (where 20,000 are on strike at this time); let us pray God to bring peace to the hearts of Queen and people and the gift of reconciliation to resolve all our wounding conflicts.
Lord in your mercy,
    Hear our prayer.

Let us pray God, through Jesus Christ our Lord, to prosper the work of ecologists, to give wisdom to all who harvest the resources of land and sea, to protect the harvesters when they reap wisely and to restrain them when they exploit foolishly. Let us pray God to look favourably upon all agencies that combat hunger especially Christian Aid in which we share, and to feed the hungry.
Lord in your mercy,
    Hear our prayer.

Let us remember before God the great company of sufferers and those who try to help them. Let us remember particularly the prisoners of conscience and Amnesty International which champions their cause. Let us commend to God's keeping all whom we love and pray that he will grant to them and to all for whom we have prayed the peace that is from above. Lord in your mercy,

Hear our prayer.

Commemoration

We remember with gratitude before you, O God, those who have fallen on the gentle sleep of death and rest in the faith of Christ. We rejoice in hope of the waters of comfort and the paradise of joy, the place whence all sorrow and sighing and weeping have fled away in the light of the saints. Make us worthy we pray you to inherit with them those good things beyond our seeing, beyond our hearing, beyond our imagining which you have prepared for those who love you; through Jesus Christ our Lord.

SERVICE TEN

Sentences

There is one body and one Spirit, as there is also one hope held out in God's call to you; one Lord, one faith, one baptism; one God and Father of all, who is over all and through all and in all.

Here is the test by which we can make sure that we are in him. Whoever claims to be dwelling in him binds himself to live as Christ himself lived.

Adoration

Glory to God in the highest—the creative, living God by whose energy the world is constantly sustained.
Glory to the Son, the Word made flesh, who entered human life as man and died for us, that we might rise with him to everlasting life.
Glory to God the life-giving Spirit, who makes known the wonder of the Father's love, even to our hardened hearts.
Glory be to God the Trinity, our inspiration, our fulfilment and our destiny in Jesus Christ our Lord.

Confession and Absolution

Lord God, we come before you in great need of your forgiveness and your cleansing. We acknowledge the impurity, the lack of true commitment, in our daily living. Whatever other people may be generous enough to think, you know too well just how far we have fallen short. Sometimes our sin is the result of conscious and deliberate decision; sometimes it is caused by our dullness and our lack of vision. Even our acts of service become tainted by self-centredness and pride; but the mixed motives that we hide from others

are not hidden from you. Father, in your mercy
pardon us, and make us whole again.

Jesus said: Go in peace. Your sins are forgiven.
For this assurance of forgiveness and the promise of
renewal, we give thanks to you, almighty God.

Supplication

Help us to live this week truly in the Spirit of our
risen Lord—bringing his values and his attitude to
bear on all our decisions and on all of our relationships; and to Jesus, with the Father and the Spirit,
be honour and glory for ever.

Thanksgiving

Almighty God, we bless you for the truth and love
revealed in Jesus Christ—for his power to bring whole-
ness into broken lives, and to give peace where there
had been fear and turmoil. We bless you for his
sharing of our daily life, his offering on Calvary, his
resurrection, and the constant presence of his Spirit
now within the church, his body. We thank you too
for daily gifts—the joy of friends and families—beauty,
colour, rhythm in the world of nature—food and
drink—and the discoveries and possibilities that have
been opened up within our generation.

Dedication

Eternal God, in dedicating these gifts to the service
of Christ's church, we dedicate also ourselves; and
pledge that we will live this week in the service of
Christ, and in the strength of the help the Holy Spirit
gives us.

Intercession

We offer intercession for the church of Christ on earth, and ask your guidance for the kirk in Scotland— that its ministers and office-bearers may be open to the leading of the Spirit, and its congregations may be shown how to mediate the hope and healing of our Saviour. We remember those who work as missionaries overseas, especially our own partners ... and all those who work for greater justice in the world's use of its resources.

We intercede also for our country: for our Queen, our government, our local councillors; for people who have lost their jobs, and those whose livelihood is insecure; for the victims of violence, and for those who commit violence. Grant, Lord God, that soon we may see signs of spiritual re-awakening, which will lead our nation to more settled and contented times.

We bring before you all those dear to ourselves, and those of our community, who are passing through hard times or finding their faith tested—the ill . . . the lonely . . . the depressed . . . and the bereaved. . . . Let your healing restore them and your love console them, and our friendship be used to help them; through Jesus Christ our Lord.

Communion of Saints

We thank you for the hope that is ours in Christ— the hope of the world as it shall one day be, and hope of the life beyond this world where your people rejoice in your presence without ceasing. Help all of us to live usefully and profitably in this world of time, that when we are taken from it we may be found fit by

grace for the world of eternity. All our prayers we offer in the name of Jesus Christ the church's king and head, to whom with the Father and the Spirit be honour, glory, dominion and power, world without end.
Our Father . . .

SERVICE ELEVEN

Sentences

God shows his love for us in that while we were yet sinners Christ died for us.

Therefore, being justified by faith, we have peace with God through our Lord Jesus Christ.

Adoration

Almighty God, the giver of all life and breath and hope, we worship and we glorify your holy name. The whole creation has come into being through your power; and we rejoice that your purpose for creation is a loving purpose. You revealed your love for us in Jesus Christ; and we are privileged indeed who have been brought to a living faith in him. With his people in each corner of the world we join our offering of worship to the offering that rises to you constantly from earth and heaven. Blessing and honour and glory and power be to our God—Father, Son and Spirit— on this day and always; through the priesthood of our Saviour Jesus Christ.

Confession and Absolution

We acknowledge, Lord God, our share in the world's shortcomings and its tensions. We are wayward creatures, who cannot even love the people closest to us as we want to love them; and we know our lives have been distorted by self-centredness and by our weak priorities.

Father, grant us your forgiveness and your healing. Straighten our confusion and bestow on us again the Holy Spirit—so that our energies may be more truly harnessed to your will; through Jesus Christ, who died for our forgiveness.

Supplication

Lord Jesus, you have given us our freedom as God's sons and daughters. It is through your suffering that we have been liberated. Save us from taking that suffering for granted. When we grow cold in faith or slack in service, help us to remember just how much we owe to you and to the loving mercy of the Father; and inspire us, day by day and year by year, to make a more realistic response. Make us more like you. We offer all our prayers to the Father in your name.

Thanksgiving

Eternal God, we praise you for your relevation to us in Jesus your Son—the friend of sinners and unlovely souls. We praise you for the blessings of the world's redemption, for the saving work of Christ, and for the possibilities he opened up to us. At every stage of life and during every day of life we are surrounded by the blessings you have given us. For all of them in their variety and generosity we bless you and we praise your holy name.

Dedication

We bring our gifts to you, Lord God, in gratitude and hope. In dedicating them, we dedicate ourselves again to be your people in the world, in the strength and the enabling power of Jesus Christ our Lord.

Intercession

We offer prayer for the church of Jesus Christ in all her branches and traditions—that through her witness and integrity the whole world may see and believe. We pray for our own congregation—that the part we play within our own community may be one that truly reflects Christ. We pray for those who have no faith by which to live; and for the people who did once have faith, but now feel overwhelmed by doubt or disappointment.

Bring new peace to your divided family, Lord our God: a peace in which the strong will recognise responsibility towards the weak, the rich towards the poor; a peace in which all races can accept each other and respect each other; peace that reaches down into the hearts and lives of men. Give guidance to our Queen and government, and to all who hold positions of strong influence within our country. We ask you to enfold with your love those who are suffering: the ill, the anxious, the bereaved, the lonely: and we pray to you for people we know who are in special need of help. . . . Give peace and hope and healing to them all, according to their need; through Jesus Christ our Lord.

Communion of Saints

For men and women who have worked across the centuries and who built up the church in big ways and in little ways, we give you thanks. We pray that we may pass on to our children a heritage as rich as we ourselves received; and that by grace we may come at last to life within the fullness of your kingdom. Our Father . . .

SERVICE TWELVE

Sentences

Rejoice in the Lord. Sing unto him a new song. For the word of the Lord is right; and all his works are done in truth.

Adoration

Lord God Almighty, who, in the beginning, by thy Word didst create the light, send forth thy light and truth to be guides unto us.

Lord Jesus Christ, the Light of the world, deliver us from our darkness and let us see thee, the Truth.

Holy Spirit of God, guide us into all the truth, and assure us that we are children of God.

Holy and blessed Trinity, Father, Son and Holy Spirit, one God, we worship and adore thee in thine eternal glory, majesty and truth, with all thy church in heaven and earth; through Jesus Christ our Lord.

Confession and Absolution

Almighty God, blessed and holy Trinity, we confess that we have shared in the sin of men. We have turned away from the light of thy glory in the face of Jesus Christ. We have sought security in the darkness of our own thought and the ways of men. We are slow to learn that the blind cannot lead the blind. Look upon us and lighten our darkness we beseech thee.

Lord have mercy upon us.

Christ have mercy upon us.

Lord have mercy upon us.

May the almighty and merciful God grant you pardon, absolution and remission of all your sins; through Jesus Christ our Lord.

Collect for the Day

Almighty and everlasting God, who didst give to thine apostles grace truly to believe and to preach thy word: grant, we pray thee, to thy Church to love that word which they believed, and both to preach and receive the same; through Jesus Christ our Lord.

Intercession

Let us pray for the whole church of God.

O Lord our God, who didst give to the apostles the light of thy word and the truth of thy sacraments, continue these most precious gifts to thy whole church, that, living in their light, the darkness of our fears and prejudices may be scattered, and we may grow together into thy truth, and the unity of the body of Christ; through Jesus Christ our Lord.

Let us pray for the witness of the church here and everywhere.

O Lord our God, who didst give to us the light of the gospel that the darkness of men's sin and ignorance may be scattered, let all who hear today gladly receive and gladly share the word of life and truth; through Jesus Christ our Lord.

Let us pray for our sovereign lady the Queen and for our land.

O Lord our God, whose Son, Jesus Christ, is the Prince of Peace, grant thy Holy Spirit to our sovereign lady, Queen Elizabeth, to preserve her in thy truth, and comfort her by thy presence. Give thy wisdom to those who govern in her name, and who seek to order our common life. Give to our people the willingness to seek first thy kingdom and thy righteousness, that

all other good things may be added to us; through
Jesus Christ our Lord.
Let us pray for all in distress and trouble.
O Lord our God, who didst send thy Son to be the
light of men, the bread of life, the resurrection and
the life, look with pity on all who suffer at the hands
of men, those who are proud in human wisdom, those
who are ignorant of thy truth, those who are hungry,
those who are sick, those who are dying, and those
who are bereaved. In our own hearts we name any
such known to ourselves. *(Silence.)* Be with them and
help them; through Jesus Christ our Lord.
Let us pray for all our loved ones.
O Lord our God, whose Son came to share the
common experience of a family, united or separated,
be with all our loved ones, especially those separated
from us, and bind us together in thy love; through
Jesus Christ our Lord.

Thanksgiving

Lift up your hearts;
    We lift them up unto the Lord.

Let us give thanks unto our Lord God;
    It is meet and right so to do.

It is verily meet, right and our bounden duty that we
should at all times and in all places give thanks unto
thee, O Holy Lord, Father Almighty, everlasting God,
for all thy goodness and loving-kindness to us, and to
all men. We bless thee for our creation, preservation,
and all the blessings of this life; but above all for thine
inestimable love in the redemption of the world by our
Lord Jesus Christ. Therefore with angels and

archangels and all the company of heaven, we worship and adore thy glorious name, evermore praising thee and saying,

> Holy, holy, holy, Lord God of hosts,
> Heaven and earth are full of thy glory:
> Glory be to thee, O Lord Most High.
> Blessed is he that cometh in the name of the Lord;
> Hosanna in the highest.

Oblation

O God who hast given us our lives; O Jesus Christ who hast given thine own life for us; O Holy Spirit, the giver of new life; O holy and blessed Trinity, the giver of love and life to us the captives of sin and death; we give unto thee this our sacrifice of praise and thanksgiving, these our gifts laid on thy holy table, and ourselves for thy service; through Jesus Christ our Lord.

Intercession

Remember thy Holy Church on earth, teach her to seek first thy kingdom and thy righteousness, to labour for the food which endures to eternal life, and to persevere unto the end; through Jesus Christ our Lord.

Communion of the Saints

Almighty God, we rejoice that our Lord Jesus Christ has been raised from the dead to go and prepare a place for us in thine eternal presence. We rejoice that a great multitude, which no man could number,

surrounds his throne, including those whom we knew
and loved with whom we worshipped here on earth.
Keep us in fellowship with Christ and so with them
and the Church triumphant, and bring us at last to
take our place with them; through Jesus Christ our
Lord, who taught us to pray together saying:

Our Father . . .

*(This service was made for use on the 12th Sunday
after Pentecost, following the Joint Liturgical Group
Calendar and Lectionary (2nd year).)*

SERVICE THIRTEEN

Sentence

Give thanks to him and bless his name;
for the Lord is good and his love is everlasting,
his constancy endures to all generations.

Adoration

All praise be unto thee, O God, for thou art creator of all things in thy power and ruler of all things in thy wisdom, and yet thou art the gracious Father of thy people:

All praise be unto thee, O Christ, for in thy great love thou didst suffer death for our sins on thy cross, and yet thou has been raised up to life everlasting:

All praise be unto thee, O Holy Spirit, for thou dost come from the Father and the Son, and yet thou dost ever seek to dwell in the hearts of men and women as the power of love and truth divine.

Confession and Absolution

Father, remembering all thy goodness to us in creation and redemption, we make confession of our sins:
we have failed to trust thee as we ought, have mercy upon us;
we have found it hard to pray, and to have a sensitive compassion for others, have mercy upon us;
we have been content in selfish ways, and in hardship and loneliness have become possessed by despondent hearts, have mercy upon us.

May the almighty and merciful God grant to you, and to me, pardon for all our sins, time to better our lives, and the strength of his Holy Spirit.

Supplication

Eternal God, who hast caused us to live in a world of mystery, where many difficulties and uncertainties and temptations surround us, suffer us not to be cast down nor dismayed, but keep alive in each one of us hope and trust in thee, that our lives may indeed reflect thy peace, and we may be used in the service of others; through Jesus Christ our Lord.

Thanksgiving

Honour and praise and thanksgiving be unto thee, thou who art Father, Son, and Holy Spirit, one God blessed for ever.

We give thanks to thee, our Father God, for thy creative work in the beauty of these islands.

For signs of spring already with us, or to come—bursting buds, unfolding flowers, migrant birds flying north to nest, Easter visitors in the narrow streets, the celebration in the rose-coloured cathedral of communion, the offer of Christ's life to his worshipping people—

O Lord, how excellent is thy name in all the earth.

For summer days ahead—Orkney lochs lit by the glowing colours of the setting sun, the crofts and fields around, peaceful in the evening stillness, rich grass for grazing cattle, a few acres of waving gold, ripe for harvest—

O Lord, how excellent is thy name in all the earth.

But above all we bless thee for thy redemptive work, for the glory of Christ our Saviour, for the wonder of his cross, for the victory of his resurrection, for his continuing life with us—

O Lord, how excellent is thy name in all the earth.

Intercession

Grant us patience and sympathy, as now we seek to bring to thee our prayers for others.

Hear us for thy Church Universal; visit her with thy salvation, with increasing unity and peace; strengthen her everywhere with the mind and spirit of Jesus Christ thy Son.

Remember, O Lord, thy Church in our own land; strip her of the things that weigh her down, indifference, unbelief, half-heartedness in worship, fellowship, and service, and enable her to run with gladness the race of faith.

Uphold all who bear witness to thee, in lonely or difficult places, at home, or abroad. Grant them courage and perseverance, and trust in thee for future days.

Look in thy mercy upon nations. Send thy light and truth forth into the dark places of bitterness and war; strengthen the hands of all reconcilers, and hasten the day of peace.

We pray for our own land. Sustain and bless our gracious Queen, and all the members of her royal house. Direct with thy wisdom the Prime Minister and those who work in the high court of Parliament.

Hear us for all who serve in local government, not least for those who serve this town and this region, grant them thy light in their decision making.

Most merciful God, we bring to thee those who suffer in body, or mind, or spirit. We pray for the sick in hospital or at home, for those who are anxious for themselves or others, for those who have no work, or no future, for those who have lost their loved ones, especially for those bereaved or maimed in recent bomb attacks, for those who know a deep loneliness; draw near to all such, O God, and grant them deliverance, and hope, and comfort.

Take into thy sure keeping those whom we love, wherever they are this day; protect them from evil, and lead them in thy way.

Now we thank thee for all whom we have known and loved on earth, especially our own beloved, enable us to follow them, in so far as they followed Christ, and bring us at the last to be with them, and thee, in thy house of eternal joy.

And now unto thee, Father, and Son, and Holy Spirit, we ascribe as is most justly due, all dominion and power, world without end.

SERVICE FOURTEEN

Sentences

Who will stand up for us against the workers of iniquity? Unless the Lord had been our help, our soul had almost dwelt in silence.

But the Lord is our defence . . . and the rock of our refuge.

Approach

Almighty and merciful Father, we acknowledge thy goodness that holds our souls in life.

Lord Jesus Christ, Son of God, we acknowledge the strength of thy humanity standing against the workers of iniquity.

O Holy Spirit, we acknowledge thy power to secure to our hearts the goodness of the Father and the strength of the Son.

Blessed be God, three persons in one Trinity of love. Blessed be God.

Confession and Absolution

Father in heaven, we confess in thy presence that because of our follies and failings, because of the chaos and cruelty that bedevil our world, because of the ineptitude of our ways and the oppressive pessimism of our times, almost our souls had dwelt in silence. Seven whole days not one in seven we should recall to ourselves that thou art our defence, but the echoes of our Sunday praise are lost in the noise of the passing days. O Lord, thou lover of men's lives, we bring to thee ourselves, our sins and our failures, as to a merciful Father, who understandest all and forgivest all.

Lord have mercy.
>Christ have mercy.
Lord have mercy.

The almighty and merciful God grant unto us, being penitent, pardon and remission of all our sins, time for amendment of life, and the grace and comfort of his Holy Spirit.

Collect

O God, who knowest us to be set in the midst of so many and great dangers, that by reason of the frailty of our nature we cannot always stand upright; grant to us such strength and protection as may support us in all dangers, and carry us through all temptations; through Jesus Christ our Lord.

Thanksgiving

Praise be to thee, O God, who at the beginning didst give life to the world.
Praise be to thee, O God, that at the mid-point of time thou didst, in Christ, give new life to the world.
Praise be to thee that ever and again thou dost impart that new life to us, bringing spring out of the winter of our faithlessness and quickening to the sleepy seeds of our service.
Praise be to God.

Intercession

Let us pray God, through Jesus Christ our Lord, to bless the church, and to strengthen her with the gifts of the Spirit that she will not lose her nerve in godless times, nor underestimate the privilege of her worship,

nor shirk the task of pursuing righteousness and reconciliation of all men to God and to one another; Lord in thy mercy,
> Hear our prayer.

Let us pray God, through Jesus Christ our Lord, to bless the nations with peace and to lead them away from violence and war to policies and provisions which reflect his love;
Lord in thy mercy,
> Hear our prayer.

Let us pray God, through Jesus Christ our Lord, to show his favour to the Queen and to her house, to give understanding to her ministers and to make clear to our people the way of wholesomeness and truth; Lord in thy mercy,
> Hear our prayer.

Let us pray God, through Jesus Christ our Lord, to stretch forth his right hand in help and blessing upon the victims of war and upon the bereaved, upon those who face mental suffering because of what they have seen or endured, and upon the distressed of this world and of our own number;
Lord in thy mercy,
> Hear our prayer.

Commemoration

Almighty Father, we bless thee for that land of light and peace where thy saints rest from their labours, whither also thou art calling us. We thank thee for all dear to our hearts who by faith have reached that world. And as thou hast exalted into the heavens thy Son Jesus Christ, that he might prepare a place in the kingdom of thy glory for them that love thee, so lead and uphold us, that we may follow his most righteous steps here on earth, and may enter with him hereafter into thy everlasting rest; through Jesus Christ our Lord.

Our Father . . .

SERVICE FIFTEEN

Sentences

I was glad when they said to me, Let us go to the house of the Lord.

For my brethren and companions' sake I will say, Peace be within you.

Adoration

Almighty God whose glory the heavens are telling, the earth thy power, and the sea thy might, whose greatness all thy creatures that think and feel, everywhere proclaim: to thee belong all glory, honour, might, greatness and dominion, now and for ever. Thou makest us glad this day with the weekly remembrance of the glorious resurrection of thy Son our Lord; grant us now such a blessing through thy worship, that the days which follow it may be spent in thy service.

Confession and Absolution

O God our Father, we know and confess that our hearts are unworthy to receive thee. Day by day we have enjoyed thy gifts, but we have forgotten that thou wast the giver of them. Thou hast shown us what thou wouldst have us do, but we have not followed thy way. Thou hast spoken to us in thy Word, but we have not listened.

Lord have mercy upon us.

May the Almighty and merciful Lord grant you pardon and remission of all your sins, time for amendment of life, and the grace and comfort of the Holy Spirit.

Supplication

O Lord Jesus Christ, who wast moved with compassion for all who had gone astray, with indignation for all who suffered wrong: inflame our hearts with the burning fire of thy love, that with thee we may seek out the lost, with thee have mercy on the fallen, and with thee stand fast for truth and righteousness; both now and always. O God of all goodness, whose greatest gifts are thy simplest gifts, bestowed on all men; give us thy blessings, love and peace, and gladness of heart, health of body and mind, and the joy of serving thee.

Intercession

O Almighty God, who hast taught us to make prayers and intercessions for all men, hear us as we pray.

For thy holy Church throughout all the world. Glorify thy Son our blessed Lord in her.

For thy Church in this land; be merciful to us, O Lord, reviving, restoring and confirming.

For this parish and congregation, for the elders of the people, and all who serve thee; for the singers, the teachers, the visitors of the sick, that they may do their work with thy blessing.

For our Queen and all who rule over us that we may be led in ways of righteousness.

For peace in the world and brotherhood among all mankind.

For those who are today in distress, in trial or danger, in sorrow, or sickness or temptation.

For the aged, that they may be held in reverence, and may obtain tenderness from us and compassion from thee.

For the children, that they may grow up in godliness and today learn of thee.

Commemoration

For the good example of all thy faithful servants we give thee thanks, O Lord. In the communion of thy Holy Spirit, with thy redeemed of all ages, with our beloved who dwell in thy presence, we who serve thee on earth unite in ascribing to thee, O Father, with the Son and the Holy Spirit, all thanksgiving, honour and glory, world without end.

Thanksgiving

Almighty and most merciful Father, from whom cometh every good and perfect gift, we praise thee for all thy mercies. For thy goodness that hath created us, thy bounty that hath sustained us, thy patience that hath borne with us, and thy love that hath redeemed us, we praise thee, O God. For thy Son our Saviour, for thy Spirit our Comforter, for the Church our home, for the lives of all good and godly men, and for the hope of the life to come we praise thee, O God.

O Lord, we pray, send down thy Holy Spirit, to cleanse our hearts, to hallow our gifts, and to perfect the offering of our lives in thankfulness to thee.

Accept, O Lord, this offering of our worship, in which we unite our hearts and voices with all the people of Christ throughout the world this day, and with all the hosts of heaven, praising and blessing and adoring thy holy name for ever, through Jesus Christ our Lord, in whose words we sum up all our prayers, and say,

      Our Father . . .

SERVICE SIXTEEN

Sentences

Great is the Lord, and greatly to be praised in the city of our God, in the mountain of his holiness. Beautiful for situation, the joy of the whole earth, is mount Zion, on the sides of the north, the city of the great king.

God is known in her palaces for a refuge.

Approach

Almighty Father, in whom we live and move and have our being, still our restless hearts and quieten our anxious minds that we may recollect the glory and the nearness of thy presence and wait upon thee in adoration and in expectant faith, through Jesus Christ, who has broken down the middle wall of partition between sinners and an all-holy God.

Confession and Prayer for Pardon

Merciful Father, charge us not with the multitude of our transgressions nor with the sum of sins, for the burden of our guilt is more than we can bear. Thou hast done great things for us: we have done so little for thee. Thou hast offered us all thy love, we have kept back our hearts from thee. Forgive us now, O Father, those sins which we remember before thee and blot out even those shortcomings which we are too sinful to remember, for the sake of thy well-beloved Son who bore the sin of many and ever maketh intercession for transgressors.

Supplication

O God most glorious, in whose service is light and
love and salvation for body and for soul, lead us in thy
way, appoint unto us our task, assure us concerning
thy will for us, that we may serve thee daily and
hourly with a glad heart and dedicated will, because
thou art become our glory and our joy.

Help us to know that we are more than conquerors
through him that loved us, that laying aside every
weight and the sin which doth so easily beset us, we
may run with patience the race that is set before us,
looking unto Jesus the author and the finisher of our
faith through the same Jesus Christ thy Son our Lord.

Thanksgiving

God of all goodness and Father of all faithfulness,
we offer unto thee praise and thanksgiving for all thy
love.

For the life which thou hast given us to live in this
world, with its high privileges and responsibilities,
its fresh opportunities and enriching personal
relationships;

For the life which thou dost promise us in Christ,
begun here, perfected hereafter; for growth in grace,
for pardon and peace, for the hope of glory and for
the communion of the saints;

We thank thee heavenly Father.

Intercession

O thou who hast bidden us ask that it may be given
unto us, hear our petitions, we ask thee.

For the holy universal Church of the Lord Jesus Christ

that her witness may be strong and her service full
and wide, that through her labours the fullness of
mankind may be brought to Christ;
For thy servant Elizabeth our Queen, and for all who
throughout our realm occupy positions of authority
and responsibility that thy grace may guide and uphold
them in all things;
For the peoples of the world, white and black, com-
munist and democrat, rich and poor, that by thine
over-ruling providence they each may attain to that
sphere of usefulness which is thy purpose for them.
Raise up leaders of the people who shall be men of
peace and goodwill, because their faith is in thee.
Unto thee, O God of mercy, we lift up our hearts
in supplication for all in sorrow, sickness or distress,
especially for the aged and lonely, the unemployed
and the exiled; for handicapped children, for waifs
and strays; for those who live amid malnutrition and
disease. Send them forth help from thy sanctuary.
Purge our land, we ask thee, from corruption and
idleness; from crimes of violence and secret vice.
Teach us the true spirit of work and of leisure, and
grant us temperance in every pleasure.

Communion of Saints

Finally, of thy goodness, O Lord, bring us into that
land of eternal blessedness where saints immortal
reign and where thou thyself art all in all; through
Jesus Christ thy Son our Lord.

Prayers for the Christian Year

ALTERNATIVE PREFACES TO GREAT PRAYER

(No proper prefaces are provided in the *Book of Common Order (1979)* for the Third Order for Holy Communion. Three alternatives are provided here for the great festivals. They should be preceded by the dialogue on p. 35 and the prayer should continue with the *Sanctus* on p. 36.)

Christmas

Father Almighty and ever-living God,
We do well always and everywhere to give you thanks,
For from the beginning to the end of days
You are the eternal Lord,
Father, Son and Holy Spirit.
But at this season we thank and praise you
Because through love for us men
The Eternal Son came down in humility,
The Eternal Wisdom became a child in time.
He dwelt among us,
And we beheld his glory,
The glory of the only-begotten Son.
He took upon him our weakness and shame
That he might give to us his own splendour;
He shone for a little while in our darkness,
That we might for ever dwell with him in light;
He has not left us lonely in the midst of time,
But is ever with us through the power of his Spirit,
to govern, to inspire, and to save.
Therefore, in joyful hope of his coming again
With the Universal Church,
And with all the company of heaven

We praise you in the angels' hymn,
>Holy, holy, holy Lord, God of power and
>might, . . .

Easter

Father Almighty and ever-living God,
We do well always and everywhere to give you thanks,
for the Word that came to dwell among us.
The Light shone in darkness,
He came to his own,
And his own did not receive him,
They crucified the Lord of glory;
It was the hour and the power of darkness;
The kings of the earth set themselves in array,
And the rulers gathered themselves together,
Against you and your Son, Jesus Christ.
But it was not possible that death should hold him;
Your right hand, O Lord, is glorious in power,
Your right hand has shattered the enemy.
By his resurrection from the dead
You have given all power to him,
He lives for ever to make intercession for us;
He has given us the Spirit of sonship,
That we may call you "Abba", "Father".
Therefore with the whole creation,
That waits deliverance from bondage at the revealing
>of the sons of God,
With all the company of heaven,
And with the Universal Church,
We praise you in the angels' hymn,
Father, Son and Holy Spirit,
>Holy, holy, holy Lord, God of power and
>might, . . .

Pentecost

It is indeed our duty and our delight
Always and everywhere to give you thanks,
Almighty God, Father, Son and Holy Spirit.
Spirit of God,
Who in the hour of creation
Moved on the face of the waters,
All that is fair, all that is sacred,
All that is lovely and true
In the long history of man
has come from you
Through you prophets spoke,
By you God's people were guided;
You are the gift of the Father and the Son,
For on this day, as he had promised,
When he had taken his place
At the right hand of the Father,
He sent you forth to dwell in his people,
And to make us the children
of the most high God.
So now, in boundless joy
The whole created world
Joins with the angels
In their endless hymn of praise,

     Holy, holy, holy Lord, God of power and
       might, . . .

ADVENT

The coming of the Lord is in three tenses, but in Advent the emphasis is on the first coming at Christmas and, even more strongly, on the final coming in glory, judgement and fulfilment.

ADVENT 1

Sentences

Strengthen the weak hands, and make firm the feeble knees. Say to those who are of a fearful heart, "Be strong, fear not! Behold, your God will come with vengeance, with the recompense of God. He will come and save you."

"Blessed is the King who comes in the name of the Lord! Peace in heaven and glory in the highest!"

The Lord is good to those who wait for him. It is good that one should wait quietly for the salvation of the Lord. For still the vision awaits its time. If it seems slow, wait for it; because it will surely come, it will not delay.

Prayers

O Lord have mercy upon us when thou comest.
Have mercy upon our failure, our failure to reckon with judgement, our easy acceptance of forgiveness, our lack of a sense of urgency, our proneness to make tomorrow the day of repentance and renewal. Almighty God, have mercy upon us, reckon not our offences against us but pardon our transgressions for thy name's sake.

O Lord: keep us awake and alert, watching for your kingdom. Make us strong in faith, so we may welcome your Son when he comes, and joyfully give him praise, with you, and with the Holy Spirit.

Almighty God, you have given us the sure promise that our Lord Jesus will return to judge the earth: make us ready, we pray, for his royal coming, that we may consider daily the quality of our service and so be found faithful servants waiting and watching for our Master's return. Make us bold in our witness and grant in your mercy that many may be turned to righteousness before he comes; through Jesus Christ our Lord.

O God, who hast sent thy blessed Son into the world to be the Saviour of all men, and hast promised that he will come again, we pray thee to increase in us the spirit of watchfulness and prayer, that in the day of his appearing the lamps of our spirit may burn brightly, and we may enter with joy into the marriage supper of the Lamb; through Jesus Christ our Lord.

ADVENT 2

This Sunday has for long been associated with the gift of Holy Scripture, and especially with its witness to our Lord.

Sentence

Blessed (Happy) are those who hear the word of God and keep it.

Prayers

Almighty God, who in many and various ways hast spoken to thy chosen people by the prophets, and hast given us, in thy Son our Saviour Jesus Christ, the fulfilment of the hope of Israel: hasten, we pray, the coming of the day when all things shall be subject to him, who lives and reigns with thee and the Holy Spirit, ever one God, world without end.

Almighty and most merciful God, who hast given the Bible to be the revelation of thy great love to man, and of thy power; grant that through study of thy word, we may be stirred to penitence, lifted to hope, made strong for thy service, and, above all, filled with true knowledge of thee and of thy Son Jesus Christ.

Grant, O Lord, that in the written word, and through the spoken word, we may behold the living Word, our Saviour Jesus Christ.

Thank you, O Lord, for the Bible; for its power to create faith and to sustain it; for its ability to give us each day new vision and new power; for its capacity to reach to the roots of our inner life and to refresh them; for its power to enter into the innermost structures of mind and spirit and to fashion them anew; through Jesus Christ our Lord.

Almighty God, we bless you for the men of faith whom you inspired to write the holy scriptures; for the labours of all who have preserved, copied and translated them; for the wisdom given to those who have interpreted them; and for that measure of light and understanding you have granted to us; we pray that, learning what is your will, we may always obey you and live to your glory; through Jesus Christ our Lord.

ADVENT 3

On the third Sunday of Advent the Church tradition-ally remembers Christ's messenger John the Baptist and those messengers of our own day who are called to serve in the holy ministry.

Sentences

"Behold, I send my messenger before thy face, who shall prepare thy way; the voice of one crying in the wilderness:
Prepare the way of the Lord, make his paths straight."

How beautiful on the mountains are the feet of one who brings good news, who heralds peace, brings happiness, proclaims salvation, and tells Zion, "Your God is King".

Prayers

Raise up in your Church, O Lord, men and women of faith and vision for the work of the ministry. Be with all who teach and all who learn in our colleges; that the Church may be furnished with ministers who are filled with your Spirit and devoted to your service; through Jesus Christ our Lord.

We pray thee, O Lord, for all who preach thy word and administer thy sacraments in the name of Christ. Fill them with thy Holy Spirit that they may be strengthened in times of weakness and encouraged in moments of despair. May they uphold Christ, both by their words and in their lives, and in all things set forward thy glory, to the building up of thy Church and the salvation of men; through Jesus Christ our Lord.

Almighty God: in the wilderness of Jordan you sent a messenger to prepare men's hearts for the coming of your Son. Help us to hear the good news, to repent, and be ready to welcome the Lord, our Saviour, Jesus Christ.

O Christ our God, who wilt come to judge the world in the manhood which thou didst assume: we pray thee to sanctify us wholly, that in the day of thy coming we may be raised up to live and reign with thee for ever.

Almighty Father, whose blessed Son at his first coming brought redemption to his people, and peace to men of goodwill: grant that, when he comes again in glory to judge the world and to make all things new, we may be found ready to receive him, and enter into his joy; through the same Jesus Christ our Lord.

ADVENT 4

Sentences

"The time is fulfilled, and the kingdom of God is at hand; repent and believe in the gospel."

"Let your loins be girded and your lamps burning, and be like men who are waiting for their master."

"The night is far gone, the day is at hand. Let us then cast off the works of darkness and put on the armour of light."

Prayers

O God our heavenly Father, by the birth of your Son you have visited us with your salvation: help us in all our preparations for the Christmas festival to think more of others than of ourselves, and to show our gratitude to you for your gift beyond words, Jesus Christ our Lord.

Eternal God, through long generations you prepared a way in the world for the coming of your Son, and by your Spirit you are still bringing the light of the gospel to darkened lives. Renew us, so that we may welcome Jesus Christ to rule our thoughts and claim our love, as Lord of lords and King of kings, to whom be glory for ever.

Almighty God, who hast promised that thy glory should be revealed, and that all men should see it together: grant that as we welcome our Redeemer his presence may be shed abroad in our hearts and homes with the light of heavenly joy and peace; through Jesus Christ our Lord.

LESSONS AND CAROLS

At a service of Lessons and Carols held during Advent the following introduction may be used:

Beloved in Christ, in this Advent season of preparation, and expectation of the joys of Christmas, let us make ourselves ready to receive again the Christ-child, singing our songs of praise, and hearing from holy scripture of the God who visits and redeems his people; who, according to his promise through his prophets, has come in great humility in Jesus Christ; who will come again in glorious majesty to judge both the quick and the dead.

But first, let us pray for the needs of his whole world; for peace on earth and goodwill among all peoples. . . .

and the following scheme of Lessons may be used:

The Promise of Christ's Coming:

To Moses:	Deuteronomy xviii. 15–19
In Isaiah:	Isaiah xi. 1–10
In Micah:	Micah v. 2–4

The Coming of Christ:

The Annunciation:	St. Luke i. 26–33, 38
His Birth:	St. Luke ii. 1–12
The Word made Flesh:	St. John i. 1–14

The Promise of His Coming Again:

Be Prepared:	St. Luke xii. 35–40
The Day of His Coming:	II Peter iii. 3–13
First and Last:	Revelation i. 1–8

CHRISTMAS EVE

Sentences

Sanctify yourselves, for tomorrow the Lord will do wonders among you.

Though darkness covers the earth and dark night the nations, the Lord shall shine upon you and over you shall his glory appear. . . . The Lord shall be your everlasting light, your God shall be your glory.

Prayers

Father, long ago you sent your angels through the midnight of the sleeping world to tell the shepherds Christ was born in Bethlehem: come to our dark world, and stir our hearts to hear again their message of your love in Christ. Aided by your Spirit, may we grow in faith and understanding of your purposes, and so be moved to wonder and to praise.

O God Most High, on this night of joyful and expectant wonder, we tread again the path to Bethlehem and to the child whose birth was heralded by prophets, proclaimed by angels, and welcomed by shepherds. Open our eyes to see in him your loving purposes, and stir up within us the spirit of adoring praise.

Almighty God, in the quietness of this midnight hour, touch our understanding with thy Holy Spirit, that we may know again in true reality the wonder of thy love in Jesus Christ; and though there was no room for him in Bethlehem's inn, help us to make more room for him in our common life, that our lives may show his love, and our hearts receive his peace, for the sake of the same Jesus Christ our Lord.

CHRISTMAS DAY

Sentences

Behold, I bring you good tidings of great joy, which shall be to all people. For unto you is born this day in the city of David, a Saviour, which is Christ the Lord.

Let us now go even unto Bethlehem, and see this thing which is come to pass.

Unto us a child is born: unto us a son is given. Glory to God in the highest, and on earth peace, goodwill toward men.

The Lord hath visited and redeemed us. O come, let us adore him.

Prayers

Glory be to thee, O Christ, whose praises the angels sing, whom the heights of heaven adore.
In the miracle of thy stable-birth and in the mystery of thine incarnation thy people everywhere rejoice this day.

To thy name help us to bow the knee and all its worshipping, bow the head and all its thinking, bow the will and all its choosing, bow the heart and all its loving.

Glory be to thee, O Father, who by the birth of thy Son didst give a great light to dawn on the world's darkness.

Glory be to thee, O Holy Spirit, who hast again in these days hung forth a star in the lowly heaven of every Christian soul and seekest to lead us in the ways of humility and the paths of peace.

Blessed be God, the only God: three persons in one eternity of love.

Blessed be God for all that he is.

Blessed be God for all that he has done.

Blessed in his Church on earth and blessed in the height of heaven.

Blessed now, and blessed for evermore.

Blessed is he who cometh in the name of the Lord, whose coming hath redeemed us, whose nativity hath enlightened us, who by his coming hath sought out the lost and illuminated those who sat in darkness. Grant, O Father, that we who celebrate his nativity with deep devotion may also find the day of judgement a day of mercy. As we have known his benignity as our Redeemer may we also know his gentleness as our Judge; through Jesus Christ our Lord.

Lord Jesus Christ, born coloured and poor, welcomed by working men and kings, come to our world and heal our deep divisions, that we may be not white and black, male and female, employer and employed, but the children of God, seeing you, our Lord, in one another.

All glory to you, great God, for the gift of your Son, light in darkness and hope of the world, whom you have sent to save mankind. With singing angels, let us praise your name, and tell the earth his story, so that men may believe, rejoice, and bow down, acknowledging your love; through Jesus Christ our Lord.

CHRISTMASTIDE

Sentences

Glory to God in the highest, and on earth peace, goodwill toward men.

For unto us a child is born, unto us a son is given: and the government shall be upon his shoulder: and his name shall be called Wonderful, Counsellor, the mighty God, the everlasting Father, the Prince of Peace. Of the increase of his government and peace there shall be no end.

Arise, shine; for thy light is come, and the glory of the Lord is risen upon thee.

Jesus said, I am the light of the world: he that followeth me shall not walk in darkness, but shall have the light of life.

In this the love of God was made manifest among us, that God sent his only Son into the world, so that we might live through him.

Prayers

We bless and adore you, O Christ: Son of God, yet born of Mary; Son of God, yet our brother; eternal Word, yet a child without speech; clothed in glory, yet wrapped in swaddling bands; Lord of heaven and earth, yet lying in a manger.
We confess that we have lost our childlike innocence; we have despised what is tender and pure and corrupted ourselves with worldly opinions and ways.
Forgive us, O God, and make us like little children in faith, and hope, and love; so that we may wonder and worship at your manger throne.

Almighty God, Father of our Lord Jesus Christ, who hast sent thy Son to take upon him our nature, and hast made him to become the Son of man, that we might become the sons of God: grant that we, being conformed to his humility and sufferings, may be partakers of his resurrection; through the same Jesus Christ our Lord.

Almighty and eternal God, who didst send thine only-begotten Son that our eyes might see, our ears hear, and our hands handle the Word of life, the everlasting Christ: that which the scriptures openly declare, grant us most joyfully to believe; through the same Jesus Christ our Lord.

Almighty God, whose glory angels sang when Christ was born: tell us once more the good news of his coming; that, hearing, we may believe, and live to praise his name; through Jesus Christ our Lord.

Great God of power, we praise you for Jesus Christ, who came to save us from our sins. We thank you for the prophets' hope, the angels' song, for the birth in Bethlehem. We thank you that in Jesus you came to share our human life to the full, sharing its hurts and its pleasures. We give you glory for your wonderful love; through Jesus Christ, the Lord of lords and King of kings.

Intercession

Let us pray God, through Jesus Christ our Lord, to teach the Church true humility, bestowing upon her the mind and spirit of the Christ of Bethlehem that she may do her authentic part in leading men to their true greatness.

Hear us, Lord.
>Lord, hear our prayer.

Or

Lord in thy mercy
>Hear our prayer.

Let us pray God, through Jesus Christ our Lord, to enlighten the counsels of the nations fulfilling the promise of Immanuel, God with us, teaching men to honour the dictates of conscience, to forsake Herod's ways of violence and inhumanity and to pursue with single-mindedness the prize of peace.

Hear us, Lord.
>Lord, hear our prayer.

Or

Lord in thy mercy
>Hear our prayer.

Let us pray God, through Jesus Christ our Lord, to direct the searchings and seekings of wise men of our day and to teach them reverence and wonder before the majesty and mystery of all God's works and ways.

Hear us, Lord.
>Lord, hear our prayer.

Or

Lord in thy mercy
>Hear our prayer.

Let us pray God, through Jesus Christ our Lord, to enrich the homes of our land this day with love and friendship and to stablish the hearts of the faithful with courage and patience to follow wherever God is leading and to keep the way of righteousness to the end.

Hear us, Lord.
>Lord, hear our prayer.
Or
Lord in thy mercy
>Hear our prayer.

We join with God's whole church in our prayers for the world and its people.

Almighty God, your angels' song was Peace on earth, yet in your children's waywardness the peace men long for remains a dream still unfulfilled, and violence and cruelty mock the Christmas music: we pray again for peace among men, for an end to feuds and conflicts, for reconciliation between people of different race and colour, for restraint of those who would use violence to advance their cause.

You guided wise men from the east: we pray for men of wisdom and learning now in our time, for men of science and research, for those who apply new discoveries to daily life; for all who love the good earth, and seek to save it from waste and from pollution; for those skilled in economics and finance, for all who seek to increase harvests: that the knowledge and wisdom of our time be laid at the Christ-child's feet in humble offering.

Father, we remember that for the Christ-child in his nativity there was no room. Receive to your sure care all who are shut out from human love and hospitality: the homeless and the lost, the victim of persecution, the sad and the lonely, the anxious and the perplexed, the stranger and the captive: receive them all to yourself, that they may know themselves at home in your great love.

These things we pray through Jesus Christ our Lord.

LENT

Sentences

We have not a high priest who is unable to sympathise with our weaknesses, but one who in every respect has been tempted as we are, yet without sinning. Let us then with confidence draw near to the throne of grace, that we may receive mercy and find grace to help in time of need.

The Lord is good to those who wait for him, to the soul that seeks him. . . . Let us test and examine our ways, and return to the Lord.

Jesus then said to his disciples, "If anyone wishes to be a follower of mine, he must leave self behind; he must take up his cross and come with me."

Come now, and let us reason together, says the Lord; though your sins are like scarlet, they shall be as white as snow.

Prayers

Lord, bless to me this Lent.
Lord, let me fast most truly and profitably,
      by feeding in prayer on thy Spirit:
      reveal me to myself in the light of thy holiness.
Suffer me never to think
      that I have knowledge enough to need no
      teaching,
        wisdom enough to need no correction,
        talents enough to need no grace,
        goodness enough to need no progress,
        humility enough to need no repentance,
        devotion enough to need no quickening,
        strength sufficient without thy Spirit;
      lest, standing still, I fall back for evermore.

Shew me the desires that should be disciplined,
    and sloths to be slain.
Shew me the omissions to be made up
    and the habits to be mended.
And behind these, weaken, humble and annihilate in
    me self-will, self-righteousness, self-satisfaction,
    self-sufficiency, self-assertion, vainglory.
May my whole effort be to return to thee;
        O make it serious and sincere
        persevering and fruitful in result, by the help
            of thy Holy Spirit and to thy glory, my Lord
            and my God.

O God, whose love we cannot measure nor ever
number thy blessings; we bless thee for all thy goodness, who in our weakness art our strength, in our
darkness, light, in our sorrows, comfort and peace,
and from everlasting to everlasting art our God,
Father, Son and Holy Spirit, world without end.

God of eternity, in whose image we have been created,
we lift up our hearts to you with wonder and with
hope. You have called us to be your people—your
representatives within the world. It is a task too great
for us to bear in our own strength; but we bless you
for the Holy Spirit who can make good what is lack-
ing in us. Let him come upon us now, to inspire our
worship and renew our dedication; in the name of
Jesus Christ our Lord.

We come before you, Father, knowing how many
compromises and betrayals spoiled our service during
the past week. With shame we look back on the record
of our unkind speech . . . our cowardly silences . . .
our weak decisions. . . . For the wrong we have

committed and the worthwhile things that we have not done, Lord God pardon and absolve your people now; through Jesus Christ our Lord.

Lord Jesus—our light and our strength and our friend —teach us the secret of the courage you found in the wilderness. Save us from being too concerned with our material needs. Keep us strong against all compromise with evil. Grant that we may never put God to the test, by presuming on his goodness. Teach us to use our energies and talents in the right ways: and with your integrity and dedication to inspire us, give us such a true devotion to the will of God that we will take up our cross every day and follow in your steps.

We offer all our prayers to the Father in your name.

Blessed be the Lord our God for the great things he has done for us in Jesus Christ. We bless you, Father, for his life and death and resurrection; for his everlasting kingship; and at this time specially for his lonely endurance in the desert and his daily struggle against evil and temptation. For his knowledge of our frailty and his understanding of our needs; for his compassion when we lose our battles against evil, we are deeply thankful. We praise you, Lord God, for the countless gifts that you have given us—in Christ, in our relationships with friends and family, and in all the varied joys and encounters of our daily life.

In gratitude we look back to our fathers in the faith; and to people who have inspired us by their loyalty to Christ and by their willingness to share his suffering. Help us in our generation to follow the Master faithfully along the narrow road that leads to life;

and when this life is over, grant in your mercy that
we share his resurrection. This we ask through Jesus
Christ who is the way, the truth, the life, now and
for ever.

FOURTH SUNDAY IN LENT

(Transfiguration)

Prayers

Father,
at the transfiguration in glory of your only-begotten
    Son,
you confirmed the mysteries of faith when the
    prophets Moses and Elijah appeared with Jesus.
You foreshadowed what we shall be
when you bring our sonship to its perfection.
Grant that by listening to the voice of Jesus
we may become heirs with him,
who lives and reigns with you and the Holy Spirit,
God, for ever and ever.

O Christ, by your transfiguration you revealed the
resurrection to your disciples before your passion
began; we pray for the Church in all the difficulties
of the world: in our trials, may we be transfigured
by the joy of your victory.

O Christ, you took your friends with you and led them
    to a high mountain:
may your Church stay close to you, in the peace and
    hope of your glory.

O Christ, you led Peter, James and John down from
the mountain and into the suffering world: when our

hearts crave permanence, may we know the permanence of your love as you take us with you on your way.

O Christ, you lightened the earth, when the Creator's glory rose upon you; we pray to you for all: may the nations come to your light.

O Christ, you will transfigure our poor bodies and conform them to your glorious body; we pray to you for our brothers and sisters who are dying: that they may be changed into your likeness, from glory to glory.

Where this Sunday is observed as Mothering Sunday the following prayer may be included:

We give thanks to thee, O God, for the love shown us by our mothers, for the mother-love with which the Church enfolds us all and for Jerusalem above, the mother of us all.

FOR PASSION SUNDAY AND
HOLY WEEK

Prayers

Approach to the Cross:

 O Lord Christ, Lamb of God, Lord of lords,
  call us, who are called to be saints,
   along the way of thy cross:

  draw us, who would draw nearer our King,
   to the foot of thy cross:

  cleanse us, who are not worthy to approach,
   with the pardon of thy cross:

  instruct us, the ignorant and blind,
   in the school of thy cross:

  arm us, for the battles of holiness,
   by the might of thy cross:

  bring us, in the fellowship of thy sufferings
   to the victory of thy cross:

  and seal us in the kingdom of thy glory
   among the servants of thy cross;

 O crucified Lord;
  who with the Father and the Holy Spirit
   livest and reignest one God almighty,
   eternal, world without end.

O King of men and Master of our lives, entering into
glory by a cross, to whom all authority is given both
in heaven and upon earth: come, Lord Christ, enter
into thy kingdom; subdue the world by the power of
thy love; be known and adored to all the ends of the
earth.

HOLY WEEK

(Palm Sunday to Easter Eve)

PALM SUNDAY

When the time had come for the Lord Jesus to t
received up, he steadfastly set his face to go t
Jerusalem. Today we remember his triumphal entry ɑ
King into the holy city in accordance with prophec

Sentences

Blessed is he that cometh in the name of the Lord
Hosanna in the highest.

Prayers

Almighty God, we praise and adore you that on th
day our Lord entered in triumph into the holy city ɑ
Jerusalem, and we pray you to give us grace that w
may welcome and crown him our Lord and King fɑ
evermore, for his holy name's sake.

Holy Lord, Father almighty, everlasting God: w
thank you for your Son Jesus, who fulfilled th
prophets' words, and entered the city of Jerusaleɪ
to die for us and all men: we praise you that he enteɪ
our world as Saviour and King and calls men to obɛ
him.

MONDAY

Jesus visits the Temple, cleanses its courts of seculɑ
traffic, and declares that his Father's house is to be
house of prayer for all nations.

Sentence

I was glad when they said to me, "Let us go to th
house of the Lord."

Prayers

Almighty God, whose Son Jesus Christ cleansed the courts of thy holy house, purify our hearts from all defilement, our worship from all insincerity, and our lives from all hypocrisy, that we may become thy holy temple, a dwelling place for thy Spirit; through Jesus Christ our Lord.

Lord Jesus Christ, you cleansed the Temple courts, and taught, saying,
My house shall be called a house of prayer for all nations;
Cleanse your Church of all evil, and so sanctify it by your saving grace, that in all the world your people may offer you true and acceptable worship; for your name's sake.

TUESDAY

Jesus teaches in the courts of the Temple, replies to the cunning questions of his enemies which they had framed to entangle him and speaks great parables of judgement and salvation.

Sentences

Jesus said: I have not spoken on my own authority: the Father who sent me has himself given me commandment what to say and what to speak.

Jesus said: You call me Teacher and Lord; and you are right, for so I am.

Prayers

Lord Jesus Christ, we remember that, as on this day, thou didst endure the contradiction of sinful men, who entered into controversy with thee; save us from the subtleties of unprofitable dispute and teach us to be meek and lowly in heart, to be gentle, patient and true that when thou comest to judge the world, we may hear thy welcome: "Come, ye blessed of my Father, inherit the kingdom prepared for you."

O God, you sent your Son our Saviour Jesus Christ to redeem the world and to teach us the way of holiness. In his name, we pray you to give to all teachers and students the love of that which is worth loving, the knowledge of that which is worth knowing, and a right judgement in all things; through Jesus Christ our Lord.

WEDNESDAY

Jesus remains in Bethany, preparing himself for the ordeal awaiting him in Jerusalem. A woman anoints his head with precious ointment, symbolically anticipating his coming death and burial. Meantime, in Jerusalem, Judas is bargaining with the religious authorities to betray his master.

Sentences

Truly my heart waits silently for God; my deliverance comes from him.

In returning and rest you shall be saved; in quietness and in trust shall be your strength.

Thou anointest my head with oil, my cup overflows. Surely goodness and mercy shall follow me all the days of my life.

Prayers

Almighty God, we remember your Son seeking strength in your presence for the trial of his faith, and the comfort he drew from being anointed by his friend, and we pray for faith to look to you, that we may find strength to do your will and courage to meet death unafraid.

O God, who for our sakes didst suffer thy Holy One to be sold for thirty pieces of silver: make us so mindful of the great price wherewith thou hast bought us, even the precious blood of thy dear Son, that we may never, even to gain the whole world, betray thy merciful great kindness; nor him who now liveth and reigneth with thee and the Holy Ghost, one God, world without end.

THURSDAY

Jesus meets with his disciples in the Upper Room at Jerusalem, washes their feet, gives the New Commandment, institutes the Holy Supper, makes the Great Intercession, and then goes out to his Agony, in the Garden of Gethsemane, where he is betrayed and arrested.

Sentences

Jesus said: I am the living bread which came down from heaven; if any one eats of this bread, he will live for ever.

You are my friends, if you do what I command you.

I give you a new commandment: love one another; just as I have loved you, you also must love one

another. By this love you have for one another, everyone will know that you are my disciples.

Prayers

The feet washing

Almighty God, who didst disclose the secret of pre-
cedence in thy kingdom, when hands that had
fashioned the world washed the disciples' feet: put
away from us all pride of place and possession that
we may find joy in serving our brethren in season and
out of season, after the example of our Lord, who
liveth and reigneth with thee and the Holy Ghost, one
God, world without end.

Son of Man, who on the night before your passion
took towel and water and washed the feet of your
disciples: give us understanding of what you have
done, and teach us to follow the example of your
humility, that by love we may serve one another for
love of you, our Saviour and our Lord.

The Lord's Supper

Lord, this is thy feast, prepared by thy longing, spread
at thy command, attended at thine invitation, blessed
by thine own word, distributed by thine own hand,
the undying memorial of thy sacrifice upon the cross,
the full gift of thine everlasting love, and its perpetu-
ation till the end of time. Lord, this is bread of
heaven, bread of life, that whoso eateth, never shall
hunger more. And this the cup of pardon, healing,
gladness, strength, that whoso drinketh, thirsteth not
again. So may we come, O Lord, to thy table. Lord
Jesus, come to us.

Lord Christ, we recall at this time how you met with your disciples in the upper room and hallowed bread and wine as the memorials of your body and blood. We thank you for this sacrament of our redemption and for all that it reveals to us of your love; and we pray that whenever we meet at your table to obey your command, "Do this in remembrance of me", we may know your risen presence in our midst and feed upon you, the true bread from heaven, till we come to your everlasting kingdom.

The Agony in the Garden

Be thou ever blessed, O Lord Christ, for thy sovereign mercy; who, though assailed by loneliness, and a dread agony, didst choose to obey the Father's will even to death for our redemption, and make both earth and heaven rejoice; and now reignest, the First and the Last and the Living One, God, for ever and ever.

Lord Jesus Christ, in Gethsemane you shared our human feelings of loneliness and desolation; we praise you that even in this agony you willed to believe and to obey, so that the triumph of Easter became yours by right and ours by grace.

Note: This day is often called "Maundy" Thursday. "Maundy" is derived from the Latin "mandatum" (= command) and refers to the "New Commandment" to love one another which Jesus gave to the apostles at the Last Supper on this Thursday, the night before his death (John 13.34).

GOOD FRIDAY

Jesus is examined and tried by the Sanhedrin and is condemned to death for blasphemy. He is hurried before the Roman Procurator, and, after being mocked and scourged, is sentenced to death on the charge of treason, the sentence being carried out by crucifixion. He speaks the Seven Words from the cross, and, at three o'clock in the afternoon, he dies.

Sentences

God shows his love for us in that while we were yet sinners Christ died for us.

Behold, the Lamb of God who takes away the sin of the world.

I, when I am lifted up from the earth, will draw all men to myself.

Prayers

O Lord Jesus Christ, Son of the living God, we pray thee to set thy passion, cross and death between thy judgement and our souls, now and in the hour of our death. Grant mercy and grace to the living, rest to the dead, to thy holy Church peace and concord, and to us sinners everlasting life and glory; who with the Father and the Holy Spirit livest and reignest God world without end.

Living God, whose Son died on the cross for every one; show us, by his dying, how the place of defeat can be the place of victory; and help us so to bear our own cross, that men and women may recognise in us the victory of your grace.

EASTER EVE
Jesus' body lies in the tomb until the resurrection.

Sentences

Rest in the Lord, and wait patiently for him.

I have set the Lord always before me: he is at my right hand and I shall not fall. Therefore my heart is glad and my spirit rejoices: my flesh also shall rest secure. For you will not give me over to the power of death: nor suffer your holy one to see corruption.

Prayers

O God, in baptism we share in the death of your Son our Saviour; give us true repentance that we pass with him through the grave and gate of death, and be reborn to new life in joy, through him who died, was buried, and who rose for us, Jesus our Lord.

It is meet and right, holy Father, almighty, eternal God, at all times to give praise to thy goodness; but on this night and day the more abundantly, from souls exulting in joy. For this night is the mother not of darkness but of light, whereon day rose for ever; even our resurrection, the Lord Jesus Christ.

Father we praise you that by our Lord's rest in the tomb of Joseph he has sanctified the grave and robbed it of its finality. In your mercy bless those who mourn this day, who have stood by the grave (resting place) of a loved one. May they know that the Saviour has passed by even here to disperse the shadows, and so may they be drawn into a bright and confident hope. May the memorials of their dead hold for them no fear or regret but stand only for good and wholesome memories, pointing forward to the resurrection of the body on the day of our Lord's return.

Lord Jesus Christ, your sacrifice brought liberation to the living and the dead. By your victory the whole creation was redeemed. We thank you for the hope we have, that none who has died is beyond the reach of your love. Trusting in the coming resurrection, we look gratefully and humbly to your empty cross, and bless you for the good news that reverberated from it to the deepest corners of the universe.

Father, into thy hands we commend ourselves, our souls and bodies; into thy hands we commend our dear ones, near or far away; in the companionship of thy Son Jesus Christ and in the power of his Spirit, we commend into thy hands all we have and are; Abba, Father into thy hands.

EASTER DAY

Salutation

Alleluia. Christ is risen.
>He is risen indeed.

Sentences

Christ our Passover is sacrificed for us: therefore let us keep the feast.

Christ is risen from the dead, and become the first fruits of them that slept. For since by man came death, by man came also the resurrection of the dead. For as in Adam all die, even so in Christ shall all be made alive.

Thanks be to God, who gives us the victory through our Lord Jesus Christ.

Fear not, I am the first and the last, and the living one; I died, and behold I am alive for evermore.

Prayers

Praise be to the God and Father of our Lord Jesus Christ, who in his great mercy gave us new birth into a living hope by the resurrection of Jesus Christ from the dead. Praise be to Jesus the Son, the Lamb of God, who has taken on himself all the sin of the world, and is risen this day to everlasting life and glory. Praise be to God the Holy Spirit, who raises us to new life with Christ. Praise and thanks and blessing be to God the King and Saviour of creation, on this day of victory and light.

Almighty Father, it is through your mercy we can come with joy to greet the risen Christ, and not through any merit in ourselves. We know that we are guilty of the very sins that drove him to the cross—disloyalty and cowardice . . . jealousy and twisted thinking . . . wrong values and shortsighted vision. . . . Father, in the love that radiates from Jesus' empty cross, forgive: then raise us up on to the level of a new and finer life, in Christ. Let the joy of Christ-alive reach deep down into us, the recollection of Christ-crucified dictate our values and our thinking and our speaking—till our actions and our attitudes are purified, and Christ is reflected in us.

Lord Jesus, as you made yourself known first at Easter to the people who most loved you and missed you, make yourself known on this Resurrection day to any who have felt cut off from you—any who are burdened by guilt, and do not understand how much you love them—any who feel that joy has gone out of their life for ever. And as you dealt patiently with the problems of Thomas, deal patiently too with all people who are handicapped by closed minds—all who fear that the resurrection news is too good to be true—all who are held back from faith by intellectual barriers of doubt. Make yourself known to them too; and set them free.

O thou true sun of the world, ever rising and never going down; who by thy brightness dost nourish and gladden both heaven and earth; mercifully shine into our hearts; drive away the mists of error and the dark night of sin, that we may all our life walk as in daylight, may be pure and clean from the works of darkness, and may do all the good thou hast planned for us in the purposes of thy love.

We bless thee, O God, for the unwonted light that was brought to the world through the resurrection of thy

Son, shattering the horror of grey and hopeless days. We bear witness to the glory of thy mighty works, for thou didst make the day of things that pass radiant with a light that is eternal. Father receive the supplications that rise to thee from thy praying people. Strengthen us. Grant us the gifts of hope and peace in our hearts through Jesus Christ our Lord.

Show us, O God most holy, according to the measure of our mortal sight, the glory of the risen Christ, for as the rising sun breaks upon the night shadows and day leaps into joy, so has Christ overcome the powers of darkness and of death, and has disclosed to us the wonders of your power and love.

Truly, you have risen, O Lord! Let the gospel trumpets speak, and the news as of holy fire, burning and flaming and inextinguishable, run to the ends of the earth. You have risen, O Lord! Let all creation greet the good tidings with jubilant shout; for its time of release has come, the long night is past, the Saviour lives! and rides and reigns in triumph now and throughout all the ages.

EASTER AND ASCENSION

Sentences

This is the day which the Lord has made. We will rejoice and be glad in it.

Rejoice in the Lord always, and again I say, rejoice.

Lift up your heads O ye gates: be ye lifted up ye everlasting doors, and the King of glory shall come in.

Let the heavens be glad and let the earth rejoice, and let men say among the nations, the Lord is king.

Seeing then that we have a great high priest, that is passed into the heavens, Jesus the Son of God, let us come boldly unto the throne of grace, that we may obtain mercy, and find grace to help in time of need.

Blessed be the God and Father of our Lord Jesus Christ, which according to his abundant mercy hath begotten us again unto a lively hope by the resurrection of Jesus Christ from the dead, to an inheritance incorruptible, and undefiled, and that fadeth not away, reserved in heaven for you.

Prayers

Praise and honour, glory and might, to him who sits on the throne and to the Lamb for ever and ever. Praise and glory to the ever-living God, who has created us in love and offered us in Christ the hope of life and joy unending. To our Maker and our Father we present the worship of our hearts and of our lives. Let the Spirit of the risen and ascended Christ be with us to unite our offering of praise with the offering that rises from the Church around the world and from the hosts of heaven.

Lord Jesus Christ, our king: rejoicing in your victory, we thank you that good is a greater power than evil. Lord Jesus Christ, our friend: rejoicing in your sharing of our life, we thank you for your constant intercession for us now. Lord Jesus Christ, our priest: rejoicing in the new way you have opened up for us on Calvary, we thank you that we can approach the throne of God in full assurance of our faith. Lord Jesus Christ, our judge: rejoicing in the love you have for all mankind, we thank you that we have no cause to be afraid. The present and the future, and all of eternity, belong to you. Save us and strengthen us, and bring us by grace into your kingdom.

Almighty and everlasting God, who didst raise thy Son Jesus Christ from the dead and set him upon the glorious throne of thy kingdom giving him a name that is above every name, we worship and adore thee in the fellowship of thy redeemed, ascribing to thee blessing and honour and glory and power, for ever and ever.

Praise be unto thee O Christ, who art ascended to thy Father's right hand on high, and hast opened for us a new and living way into the holiest of all. Praise be unto thee who art exalted in great power and glory. Praise be unto thee who art king and head of the Church and high priest over the house of God.
By thy sacrifice upon the cross, forgive our sins.
By thy resurrection from the dead, raise us up to newness of life.
By thy mighty intercession for us at the right hand of the Father, strengthen and protect us with thy heavenly aid.

Blessing and honour and glory and power be unto him that sits upon the throne, and to the Lamb for ever.

O Lord Jesus Christ, whom men saw on the mountain top transfigured with the splendour of God; Lord Christ, whom they saw at thy ascension girt about with the light of heaven, thy pierced hands stretched out in blessing over the world: open our eyes to see thee as thou art, and help us so to know thee that we may love thee and the world which thou didst come to save.

O Christ whose wondrous birth meaneth nothing unless we be born again, whose death and sacrifice nothing unless we die unto sin, whose resurrection nothing if thou be risen alone: raise and exalt us, O Saviour, both now to the estate of grace and hereafter to the state of glory: where with the Father and the Holy Spirit thou livest and reignest, God for ever and ever.

O risen Saviour, bid us rise with thee and seek those things which are above, not only seek, but set our whole heart upon them. Thou art in heaven, O Christ, ever raising lives to thyself: by thy grace may our lives be making that ascent not in dream but in truth, not now only but tomorrow and all the days of our lives. Give us eyes to see thee on the throne, thou King reigning in holiness, thou conqueror of all evil, thou majesty of love, very God and very man, of glory unimaginable and eternal, in whom all hope is sure.

Lord Jesus Christ, ascended and hidden from our sight, yet really present to our faith, we acknowledge you to be Saviour of the world and King of the new creation. Above our weakness and despair, above our strife and disunity, above our sin and rebellion, above the impersonal forces which threaten to crush us, you rule. Your love reigns supreme and can bring hope and peace and pardon and freedom. In our need of these gifts, we look to you. Lord Jesus Christ, alive for ever, lifted high over all, unlimited by time or space, universal king, we worship and adore you.

ROGATION SUNDAY

(5 after Easter)

Sentences

He that goes forth weeping, bearing the seed for sowing, shall come home with shouts of joy, bringing his sheaves with him.

As the rain cometh down, and the snow from heaven, and returneth not thither, but watereth the earth and maketh it bring forth and bud, that it may give seed to the sower and bread to the eater, so shall the Lord's word be that goeth forth out of his mouth.

Jesus said, Truly, truly, I say to you, unless a grain of wheat falls into the earth and dies, it remains alone; but if it dies, it bears much fruit.

I will cause the rain to come down in its season, saith the Lord. And the tree of the field shall yield its fruit, and the earth shall yield her increase, and they shall be secure in their land; and they shall know that I am the Lord.

Prayers

Almighty God, the source of all good, we commend unto thee the labours of men in tilling the soil and sowing the seed, and pray that thou wouldst grant favourable weather, for the springing of the seed and its growth to a rich harvest, through Jesus Christ our Lord.

Almighty God, we pray that the seed sown in the earth may grow and yield richly, and that the word, cast like seed on the soil, may be accepted in the hearts of its hearers, and bear fruit in their lives, through Jesus Christ our Lord.

It is indeed our duty and delight always and everywhere to give you thanks and praise, Almighty God, Creator of all the marvellous universe. At this time we thank you for setting us on this good earth, for supplying seed springing into growth, for endowing with patience, skill and understanding those who till the soil and reap its harvest. Above all we thank you for Jesus Christ who is the Bread of Heaven given that we may have eternal life. Therefore with angels and archangels etc.

PENTECOST

Sentences

God's love has been poured into our hearts through the Holy Spirit which has been given to us.

When we cry, "Abba! Father!" it is the Spirit himself bearing witness with our Spirit that we are children of God.

It shall come to pass, saith the Lord, that I will pour out my spirit upon all flesh.

Wilt thou not revive us again, O Lord, that thy people may rejoice and be glad in thee?

Prayers

Come, Holy Spirit, and fill the hearts of your people with the fire of your divine love. Father Eternal, send forth the Spirit and we shall be remade; and you will renew the face of all things; through Jesus Christ our Lord.

O Holy Spirit, who as a mighty wind came to the company of the apostles, drive from us now the darkness of sin, and clothe us with the light of thy glory. Come, Holy Spirit, come. Fulfil the promise of our Saviour Jesus Christ our Lord.

Almighty God, all-seeing and all-holy, we have sinned against you through wilfulness and unbelief. We have not sought light through your Spirit of wisdom. We have not sought strength through your Spirit of power. Holy Father, you sent your Spirit to convince of sin and lead to righteousness; bring us to repentance who now confess our faults before you. Grant us the peace of the forgiven, and teach us no more to grieve your Holy Spirit; through Jesus Christ our Lord.

Almighty and most merciful Father, we have not used to your glory the gifts you bestowed in sending down the Holy Spirit upon your Church. We have not remained in the grace of the gospel. We have despised your holy word spoken to us by your prophets; we have disobeyed your commandments delivered to us by your apostles. We have not fulfilled the trust you committed to us, that we should call the ends of the earth to serve you, and gather for Christ your children scattered abroad. Hide your face, O Lord, from our sins, and blot out all our iniquities. Make our hearts clean, O God, and renew a right spirit within us. Do not cast us away from your presence; take not your Holy Spirit from us.

Make thy servants, O God, to be set on fire with thy Spirit, strengthened by thy power, illuminated by thy splendour, filled with thy grace, and to go forward by thine aid, and manfully having finished our course, may we be enabled happily to enter into thy kingdom.

O God, who by thy Holy Spirit at the first established a Church, and who, sanctifying it by the same Spirit, doth still preserve and govern it; hear the prayer of thy servants, and mercifully grant us the perpetual assistance of thy grace, that we may never be deceived by any false spirit, or overcome by worldly desires, but in all our doubt may be directed in the ways of truth, and in all our actions guided by thy Holy Spirit, through Jesus Christ our Lord.

O Holy Spirit of God, on the day of Pentecost you overcame the barriers of language and your messengers were able to speak to the hearts of men of many nations and draw them to you. Grant to your Church in our generation the ability to enter into the experience and thinking of men. May its message go home to their hearts and make known to them the saving love of Christ who from his cross draws all men to himself.

Biddings to intercession for Church and Nation

Let us pray God, through Jesus Christ our Lord, to send his Spirit mightily upon the Church that in her words and her works she may banish darkness and bring to birth new life upon the earth.

Hear us, Lord.
> Lord, hear our prayer.

Or

Lord in thy mercy
> Hear our prayer.

Let us pray God, through Jesus Christ our Lord, to gather the nations to himself in closer unity, in mutual understanding, in compassion, in freedom and without fear.

Hear us, Lord.
> Lord, hear our prayer.

Or

Lord in thy mercy
> Hear our prayer.

Let us pray God, through Jesus Christ our Lord, to equip the Church spiritually to meet the challenge of the times, to send the Holy Spirit upon us that we may identify clearly those things that belong to our health and salvation and may have courage to love them and defend them.

Hear us, Lord.
    Lord, hear our prayer.
Or

Lord in thy mercy
    Hear our prayer.

Let us remember gratefully in the presence of God
that his Spirit has forged in our times strong bonds
of unity among a diversity of Christians and let us
pray God not to take his Spirit from us until we display
to the whole world one mind in belief and one passion
for righteousness.

Hear us, Lord.
    Lord, hear our prayer.
Or

Lord in thy mercy
    Hear our prayer.

Benediction

May the God of hope fill you with all joy and peace
in believing, so that by the power of the Holy Spirit
you may abound in hope, and the blessing. . . .

The Almighty and most glorious Lord God, who as
on this day sent down his Spirit upon the faithful
in tongues like flames of fire, grant you the light of
his inspiration, and inflame in you the fire of his love.
The Lord Jesus Christ, who baptises with the Holy
Spirit and with fire, make you partakers of his holy
anointing, and seal you for everlasting salvation.
The Holy Spirit distribute to you his heavenly gifts,
come upon you in his glory, and live in your hearts
henceforth and for ever.

TRINITY SUNDAY

Sentences

Holy, holy, holy, is the Lord God Almighty, who was, and is and is to come.

Jesus said, I will pray the Father, and he shall give you another Comforter, that he may abide with you for ever, even the Spirit of truth.

Through Christ we have access by one Spirit unto the Father.

Prayers

God, the Father, who hast delivered us from darkness and transferred us to the kingdom of thy beloved Son,

We worship thee.

God, the Son, Jesus Christ, the image of the invisible God, the first-born of all creation, who makest us new creatures,

We worship thee.

God, the Holy Spirit, who dost lead us so that we are sons of God, fellow-heirs with Christ,

We worship thee.

God, most holy, Father, Son and Holy Spirit, eternally one God in three persons, and three persons in one God, with all the church in heaven and on earth we worship and adore thee, through Jesus Christ our Lord.

Bless us, O God, Father, Son and Holy Spirit, with the vision of thy glory: that we may know thee as the Father who created us, rejoice in thee as the Son who redeemed us, and be strong in thee, the Holy Spirit, who dost sanctify us; keep us steadfast in the faith, and bring us at the last into thine eternal kingdom where thou art ever worshipped and glorified, one God, world without end.

God the Father, hidden in glory, we thank you that you have chosen to reveal yourself to us who, by ourselves, cannot find you. We thank you for Jesus Christ your Son, who came to reveal your love and to seek and to save the lost. We thank you for the work of the Holy Spirit, enabling your Church in all ages to grasp the breadth and length and height and depth of Christ's love and to worship you in the majesty of your being, one God in three Persons.

MICHAELMAS

(29th September)

Sentences

The angel of the Lord encamps around those who fear him, and delivers them.

Do you think that I cannot appeal to my Father, and he will at once send me more than twelve legions of angels?

Prayers

Almighty God, who of thy providence wast pleased to appoint thy holy angels to be our guardians; grant that, being continually defended by their protection, we may be enabled to rejoice in their fellowship hereafter; through Jesus Christ our Lord.

Intercession (to be included with other biddings)

Let us pray God, through Jesus Christ our Lord, to speak persuasively to the heart of the Church the brave message of Michaelmastide, the unquestionable superiority of the power of good over the powers of evil, that Christian people may not fear for the future but may hold fast to their profession.

Lord in thy mercy
        Hear our prayer.

Or

Hear us, Lord.
        Lord, hear our prayer.

HARVEST

Sentences

The earth is the Lord's and the fulness thereof.

Say not to yourselves, "My own strength and energy have gained me this wealth", but remember the Lord your God; it is he that gives you strength to become prosperous.

Prove me now herewith, saith the Lord of hosts, if I will not open you the windows of heaven, and pour you out a blessing, that there shall not be room enough to receive it.

Jesus said, "I am the bread of life; he who comes to me shall not hunger".

Enter into his gates with thanksgiving, and into his courts with praise; be thankful unto him, and bless his name.

Prayers

Lord, our God, who of thy goodness, hast promised that seedtime and harvest shall not cease, and hast again provided for us of thy bounty,
　　　We worship and adore thee.

Lord Jesus Christ, Son of God, the bread of heaven, coming down from God and giving life to the world,
　　　We worship and adore thee.

Holy Spirit of God, who alone dost bring from us the harvest of love, patience and goodness,
　　　We worship and adore thee.

God, Father, Son and Holy Spirit, one in the fulness of thy love,
　　　We worship and adore thee.

Almighty God, the fountain of all goodness, who hast
once again crowned the year with thy goodness, and
given to us the kindly fruits of the earth, give us
grace to receive them thankfully, and to use them
carefully, for our own needs and for the help of
others, through Jesus Christ our Lord.

(22/12/95)

It is indeed our duty and delight always and everywhere to give you thanks and praise, Almighty God,
eternal and holy Father, but especially on this day
we thank you for once again fulfilling your promise
that, while earth remains, seedtime and harvest shall
never cease. We thank you for the regularity of the
seasons, sunshine, rain and wind, the splendour of
the trees, the colourful glory of the flowers, the fields
ripe for harvest, and the safe ingathering of fruit
and crops. We thank you for the labour, patience,
skill and diligence of those who plough and sow and
reap. We thank you that you have satisfied us with
these gifts, and that you continually feed us with the
bread of heaven, Jesus Christ, your Son our Lord.

Lord God Almighty, Creator, Saviour, Comforter,
it is right that we should continually give thanks to
you for your goodness to all men and to us.
For the sowing of the seed, its springing up, its safe
    ingathering,
for the work of frost and snow, rain and wind on the
    soil, the warmth and ripening power of the sun,
for your providential ordering of the seasons, and the
    assurance we have that harvest follows sowing and
    planting,
        We thank you, O Lord.

For the care of farmers, the skill of workers, the
    understanding, patience, labouring, watching an
    harvesting,
for those who prepare, transport and sell our food,
for our health and strength, and our hopes for day
    to come,
        We thank you, O Lord.

For the deeper riches of your grace and love, for you
Son, our Saviour, who is the bread of life, and fo
your Spirit present always to help us to produce goo
fruit in our lives, and to assure us of your fin
harvest,
        We thank you, O Lord.

Let us bless God that though our times be out c
joint his creation wears all the ancient splendours c
autumn and his promise is fulfilled for us again tha
to the end of the age seed time and harvest shall neve
cease.
Let us bless God for the vast sweep of his provisio
for men, the endless catalogue of his gifts, for th
harvests of land and sea, for oil as much as for oats
for skills as much as for sustenance. Bless the Lord
my soul, and forget none of his benefits. Truly, C
God, you are worthy of blessing. You bring food ou
of the earth and make the hearts of men glad wit
your goodness. Praise to your name for ever and
ever.

Shine thou upon us, O Lord, the one true light, tha
we may behold thy beauty in creation, thy mind in
the everlasting gospel, thy hand both in our blessing
and in our disappointments, thy presence always and

in all places, O Father, Son and Holy Spirit, God blessed for evermore.

Lord come quickly, we pray, and restore the lost harmony between God, man and creation. Bring in your kingdom that we may receive our full adoption as sons of God and the whole universe may enter into the glorious liberty of the children of God.

ALL SAINTS
(1st November)

Sentences

You are fellow citizens with the saints and members of the household of God, built upon the foundation of the apostles and prophets, Christ Jesus himself being the chief cornerstone.

Since we are surrounded by so great a cloud of witnesses, let us lay aside every weight, and sin which clings so closely, and let us run with perseverance the race that is set before us, looking to Jesus the pioneer and perfecter of our faith.

The righteous shall be had in everlasting remembrance.

Prayers

Almighty God, from whose love neither death nor life can separate us: with the whole company of the redeemed in heaven and on earth we praise and magnify your glorious name, Father, Son and Holy Spirit, one God, blessed for ever.

Almighty God, whose people are knit together in one holy church, the body of Christ our Lord, grant us grace to follow your saints in lives of faith and commitment, and to know the inexpressible joys you have prepared for those who love you; through your Son, Jesus Christ our Lord.

Come, let us adore the King of Saints.

Blessed for ever be the eternal Spirit, whose grace brings all the saints to glory.

God and his holy angels are on our side, Jesus takes our part, and his blessed saints rejoice over us. All praise and thanks to God.

The hymn "Te Deum" may also appropriately be said or sung at this season.

PRAYERS FOR
A REMEMBRANCE SUNDAY SERVICE

Approach

Our Father God, we remember before you all who have lived and died in the service of mankind, especially those who have given their lives in the service of their country. We remember their courage, their devotion to duty, and their sacrifice of life itself, so that our nation might be able to live in peace and in freedom.

Confession and Absolution

Eternal God, recalling those whom you raised up for our defence we confess that we have not been worthy of your mercies to us, or of the sufferings endured, or of the lives laid down on our behalf; still less have we been worthy of the sacrifice of your Son, our Saviour, Jesus Christ; we have sinned by our forgetfulness of you, by our lack of trust in you, by our impatience and selfishness.

May the Almighty God grant to you and to me pardon for all our sins, time to better our lives, and the strength and comfort of his Holy Spirit.

Supplication

Remembering, O Lord, today those who, in dark days, found in you their source of light, we ask you to shine into our hearts, that your Spirit of wisdom may save us from false choices, and that in your light we may see light, and in your straight path may not stumble. Remembering, O Lord, today those who, in hard times, found in you their strength, grant us such strength and such protection as may support us in all our dangers, and carry us through all our temptations. Remembering, O Lord, today those who, in hours of strain and stress, found in you their peace, grant us to be set free from restlessness and anxiety; give us the peace and power that flow from you, and in all perplexity and distress so keep us, that we, upheld by your strength, and stayed upon the rock of your faithfulness, may abide in you, now and always; through Jesus Christ our Lord.

Thanksgiving

Truly at all times and in all places we should bless and praise you, O holy Lord, Father Almighty, everlasting God. Out of primaeval chaos you have fashioned the universe to reflect your glory and man to be your child.

We praise you for Jesus Christ whom you sent to be the Saviour of the world, rescuing us from the chaos of our sin. We bless you for his suffering that was love and his cross that was salvation and for his victory that drew the sting of death and opened the way to the kingdom of heaven for all who will tread it with him.

We praise you that from that kingdom where he reigns he has sent forth the Holy Spirit to sound in our hearts the reveille of faith, to illumine with imperishable hope the long travail of mankind and to enable us to endure till he comes again.

Remembrance

And now we bless you for all your saints and faithful servants; especially this day we bless you for all who gave their lives in our nation's defence. Let the memory of their courage and endurance ever be an example to us, that we may be taught to live by those who learned to die, and bring us, at the last, to be with them and you in your nearer presence; through Jesus Christ our Lord.

ST. ANDREW

(30th November)

Sentences

All who follow the right and seek the Lord—look to the rock from which you were hewn, to the quarry from which you were dug.

If any one serves me, he must follow me; and where I am, there shall my servant be also; if any one serves me, the Father will honour him.

Jesus said to them, "Follow me and I will make you become fishers of men".

Prayers

Almighty God, as Andrew the apostle was the means of bringing Simon Peter to a knowledge of the living Christ, grant that we too may use every opportunity to share our faith with others; and as Andrew gave up his career and home to serve his Lord, grant that we too may be willing to make any sacrifice, and to renounce those things which hold us back from true commitment; in the name of Jesus Christ our Lord.

Commemoration

Almighty Father, you have blessed us with a rich inheritance; and we look back with gratitude to all who have built up the Church of Christ in our own land: the early pioneers, the saints and martyrs and reformers, and the great host of men and women who have witnessed faithfully and worked loyally in every generation. Help us to live within the light that was carried to our shores so long ago, and to continue the work done by our forefathers—that our children may enjoy a heritage of faith, and grow up in the knowledge and the love of Christ. In your mercy, bring us to the kingdom where the saints of every nation come together round the throne, to worship and rejoice in perfect fellowship; through Jesus Christ our Lord.

Prayers of intercession should include particular reference to the needs of the country. If a special service is being held for St. Andrew's Day, the prayer of Confession should also take account of failures and sins in our life as a nation.

ST. PAUL
(25th January)

Sentences

God was in Christ, reconciling the world to himself, no longer holding men's misdeeds against them and he has entrusted us with the message of reconciliation.

Now that we have been justified through faith, let us continue at peace with God through our Lord Jesus Christ, through whom we have been allowed to enter the sphere of God's grace where we now stand.

God's love has flooded our inmost heart through the Holy Spirit he has given us.

Prayers

Paul's conversion

Almighty God, in the change from Saul the Pharisee to Paul the apostle and martyr you have shown us the power of the Holy Spirit to transform human lives. We pray that the light of the risen Christ may dawn upon all those who have not yet come to faith; and we remember those known to ourselves. . . . Grant that they may recognise Christ as their Lord and their Saviour, and be born into new life through the power of the Spirit; in the name of Jesus Christ our Lord.

Paul the missionary

Almighty God, you created every race of men of one stock, and through the witness of Paul the apostle your truth was made known to the Gentiles. Bless the work of those who strive now to extend the frontiers of the new humanity in Christ. We pray for our own missionary partners . . . and we ask that through their work men and women whose world was without hope, and without God, may be brought into union with Christ. We ask this in his name.

Paul the teacher

We thank you, Lord God, for the writings of St. Paul preserved for us in Holy Scripture. Keep the Church always faithful to the truth which was Paul's inspiration; and grant that being nourished by his teaching we may come to place our confidence in Christ alone, and may be strengthened in the power of Christ against all worldliness and all untruth; through Jesus Christ our Lord.

Paul the mystic

Eternal God, in whom we live and move and have our being, we give thanks for the example of Paul's discipline and perseverance in the power of prayer. Grant that the Holy Spirit may inspire our praying, and may bring us to a deeper understanding of your will, a fuller vision of your glory, until the mind of Christ be fully reflected in our lives; through Jesus Christ our Lord.

Paul the sufferer

Almighty Father, in your wisdom you did not see fit to lift from Paul the burden of the pain which afflicted him. We pray for the people of our generation who must learn to live with pain or disability. When their prayers for healing seem to go unanswered, help them to accept that sometimes your power comes to its full strength in weakness, and that your grace is sufficient for their need. Keep them from bitterness, and from doubting your love; in the name of him who suffered cruelly for our redemption, Jesus Christ our Lord.

Paul the martyr

Almighty God, you gave to the apostle Paul a faith that made him able to endure a life of constant self-denial, danger, hardship; and a love of Christ that strengthened him to face injustice, persecution, even death itself. Grant us that same faith, and that same love—that being sustained by the hope set before us we may face all the demands of our discipleship, and take up our cross each day to follow in the footsteps of our Saviour; through Jesus Christ our Lord.

WEEK OF PRAYER FOR CHRISTIAN UNITY

(18th–25th January)

Prayers *(in traditional language)*

O God, the Father of our Lord Jesus Christ, our only Saviour, the Prince of Peace; give us grace seriously to lay to heart the great dangers we are in by our unhappy divisions. Take away all hatred and prejudice, and whatsoever else may hinder us from godly union and concord; that, as there is but one body, and one Spirit, and one hope of our calling, one Lord, one faith, one baptism, one God and Father of us all, so we may henceforth be all of one heart, and of one soul, united in one holy bond of truth and peace, of faith and charity, and may with one mind and one mouth glorify thee; through Jesus Christ our Lord.

O Lord Jesus Christ, who saidst unto thine apostles, Peace I leave with you, my peace I give unto you; regard not our sins, but the faith of thy Church, and grant her that peace and unity which is agreeable to thy will, who livest and reignest for ever and ever.

O God, the physician of men and nations, the restorer of the years that have been destroyed; be pleased to complete the work of thy healing hand; draw all men unto thee and one to another by the bonds of thy love; make thy Church one, and fill it with thy spirit, that by thy power it may unite the world in a sacred brotherhood of nations, wherein justice, mercy and faith, truth and freedom may flourish, and thou mayest be glorified; through Jesus Christ our Lord.

For prayers in contemporary language, it is recommended that use be made of the material published each year by the British Council of Churches for the Week of Prayer; and that particular intercessions be offered for talks and negotiations in which the Church of Scotland is currently engaged with other denominations.

PRAYERS FOR THE DEDICATION OF CHURCH FURNISHINGS

Order of Service

Call to worship
Praise (unaccompanied if an organ is to be dedicated)
Dedication of organ, followed by praise
Dedication of prayer desk
Prayers
Praise
Dedication of lectern
Scripture readings
Praise
Dedication of pulpit
Sermon
Creed
Praise
Dedication of alms dish or offering plates
The offerings
Dedication of font or holy table
Prayers
Praise
Dismissal and Benediction

Note: The order printed above follows, in its basic structure, that given at the beginning of this book (pp. vi and vii). It indicates appropriate points at which the dedication of various items may take place, usually immediately before that point in the service at which they would be used. It is not, of course, expected that on any one occasion there would be more than one or two acts of dedication.

At the appropriate point in the service, the minister shall proceed to that part of the church where the act of dedication is to take place. The congregation standing, one of the following prayers may be offered.

125

Lord God, all things around us have their beginning in your creating power. We praise you that you have continued to love your creation to the extent of giving your Son Jesus Christ as Saviour. In him we look for the new heaven and the new earth when all things will be free to praise their maker. As we await that day, we ask that the Holy Spirit may bless our act of dedication, that our gifts may truly witness to our faith and our hope.

or

Blessed and glorious Lord God Almighty, by whose power, wisdom and love all things are sanctified, enlightened, and made perfect; be merciful unto us and bless us, and cause thy face to shine upon us, that what we now do may please thee, and shew forth the honour of thy name; through Jesus Christ our Lord.

If that which is to be dedicated is a gift, the donor or representative may then offer the gift in such words as these:

As minister of this parish, will you receive this . . . (in the name of . . . *or*, in memory of . . .) and dedicate it to the glory and praise of God?

The minister may respond:

On behalf of the congregation I gratefully accept this gift.

The minister shall then say:

In the faith of our Lord Jesus Christ I solemnly dedicate this/these . . . and declare it/them to be set apart for use in this place, to the glory of Almighty God. In the name of the Father and of the Son and of the Holy Spirit.

Prayers

At the Dedication of an Organ

Our heavenly Father, your free gift of grace in Jesus Christ has put a new song in our mouth. We praise you that through music we can express something of the glory we have seen, the victory we share, and the joy that we know. Bless your people as they sing, that as our offering of praise is enriched by the music of this organ, so the Holy Spirit may always be present among us, lifting our song into the worship of heaven through Jesus Christ our Lord.

or

O Almighty God, we ask thee graciously to accept this organ which we have dedicated unto thee, for the honour of thy holy name, and the more worthy rendering of thy worship. Grant that by its reverent and holy use, thy praise may now and ever be set forth in thy church and that all who worship here may be led to sing with grace in their hearts unto thee; through Jesus Christ our Lord.

At the Dedication of a Prayer Desk

Give thanks to the Lord,
because he is good,
and his love is eternal.

>   Let the people of Israel say,
>   "His love is eternal."

Let the priests of God say,
"His love is eternal."
        Let all who worship him say,
        "His love is eternal."

Almighty God our Father, to whom our prayers and
the worship of the Church are addressed, receive this
prayer desk and bless its use.

Lord Jesus Christ, our great High Priest through
whom we pray, let our prayers be accepted before the
Father's throne.
Holy Spirit of God, who can make coherent even our
inarticulate groans, lift our prayers into the eternal
prayer of Jesus.
O Lord, teach us to pray:
        Our Father . . .

or

Almighty God, who art the hearer of prayer, hallow
this prayer desk which we have set apart for the service
of thy church.
O holy Father, to whom we draw near with boldness
through Jesus Christ our Lord, remember his merits
and not our unworthiness; and grant that our prayers,
being offered in his name, may be accepted for his
sake; to whom with the Father and the Holy Spirit
be all praise and glory, now and for evermore.

At the Dedication of a Lectern

We thank you Father for the rich gift of the Bible;
for historian and prophet, apostle and evangelist,

through whom you have revealed your nature, called your people to holiness, and offered new life in Christ. Send your Spirit to bring to life the words of scripture both for those who read and those who hear, that we may recognise the Word of Life himself, Jesus our Lord, as he comes among us in risen power.

or

Grant, O Lord, that all who in this place shall read thy holy scriptures may be filled with the faith of the gospel, and with thankfulness to thee may receive the Word of Life into honest and good hearts, and may bring forth fruit with patience; through Jesus Christ our Lord.

At the Dedication of a Pulpit

Almighty God, whose living word has been spoken to your people in all ages, receive this pulpit, symbol of our need and our willingness to hear that word in our own generation. Bless those who will preach. May they prepare themselves prayerfully and proclaim the gospel of Christ confidently and without fear or favour, in the power of the Holy Spirit. Bless those who will hear. May they receive the proclamation of good news thankfully and responsively, and so be strengthened in faith, hope and love.

or

Cause thy Church to arise and shine, O Lord, and let her ministers be clothed with righteousness and salvation; that thy word may not return unto thee void, but have free course and be glorified; prospering in the thing whereunto thou hast sent it, and prevailing mightily to turn people from darkness to light, and from the power of Satan unto God. By thy grace may they receive the forgiveness of sins, and an inheritance among the saints; and to thee Father, Son and Holy Spirit, one God, be honour and glory, world without end.

At the Dedication of an Alms Dish, Offering Plates, or Offering Bags

O God our Father, we praise you for mankind's supreme offering—the sacred life and death of Jesus Christ. By this sacrifice we are saved. With this sacrifice we identify. To this sacrifice we respond with our offerings.

Bless this alms dish (*or*, . . .) and help us to be responsible in our stewardship of all your gifts to us, and joyful in our devotion of the first fruits to your glory; through Jesus Christ our Lord.

or

O Lord our God, who art king of all the earth; receive, we pray, this alms dish (*or*, . . .) which we have now set apart for thy service. And accept, of thine infinite goodness, the offerings which thy people, in joyful obedience here yield and present to thee. Grant thy blessing, that these gifts being devoted to thy service, may be used for thy glory, and for the welfare of thy Church and people; through Jesus Christ our Lord.

At the Dedication of a Font

O God, your love is unconditional and your promises are never broken; we praise you for the new covenant in Jesus Christ into which we have been brought by baptism. May this font be at all times a reminder to us that we have been saved by grace. May those who are here baptised into Christ learn to walk with their Lord in newness of life; and may all the faithful who have been buried and raised up with Christ in baptism continue to know the inner presence of the Holy Spirit as the wellspring of life. Glory be to the Father, and to the Son, and to the Holy Spirit: as it was in the beginning, is now, and ever shall be, world without end.

or

O Lord God, with whom is the fountain of life; hear the prayers of thy servants, and accept and bless this font, which we have set apart to thy glory. Grant that whosoever shall here be brought unto Christ for baptism being sanctified by the Holy Spirit, and received into the ark of thy Church, may ever remain among the number of thy faithful sons and daughters. Grant, also, O Lord, that this font may ever witness to the covenant of life into which we have been admitted. Buried with Christ by baptism into death, grant, that like as he was raised up from the dead by thy glory, O Father, we may walk before thee in newness of life, and being upheld daily by thy Holy Spirit, may be made fit for the inheritance of the saints in light; through Jesus Christ our Lord, who liveth and reigneth with thee and the Holy Spirit, one God, world without end.

At the Dedication of a Holy Table

Lord God our Heavenly Father, we humbly offer
your glory this table. Here it shall stand in our mid
to be a constant reminder of that consecrated li
which was offered for us and by which alone we a
acceptable before you.

May this table point us to Christ, his birth into o
humanity; his baptism for us; his life of perfe
obedience, faith, and love, fulfilling your requiremen
of us; his entering into our death, bearing away upc
himself the sin of the world; his rising on the first da
of the week; his ascending into heaven where he pray
for us now and at all times. May this holy table poi
us to Christ, in whom you come to us, and throug
whom we present ourselves to you—a living sacrific
May your people, sharing in the body and blood c
Christ around this table be fitted for heaven, renewe
in the gifts of the Spirit, empowered for mission, an
enabled to remain always in him who is our hope c
glory; through the same Jesus Christ our Lord.

or

Almighty and eternal God; accept and bless this tabl
set apart to thy glory, to be in this church a witnes
to thy redeeming love. Grant that those who sha
partake from this holy table of the blessed sacramer
of the body and blood of Jesus Christ thy Son, ma
receive, to their great and endless comfort, the re
mission of all their sins; may be filled with thy grac
and heavenly benediction; and finally be made par
takers of his glorious resurrection unto eternal life
And grant, O God, that the prayers and offering
which thy people here present unto thee, may com

p with acceptance before thy throne; through him who stands within the veil, eternal high priest and angel and mediator of the new covenant, and who has consecrated for us a new and living way into the holiest of all, even Jesus Christ thy Son our Lord. And unto him with thee, O Father Almighty, and the Holy Spirit, one God, be all honour and glory, now and for ever.

Suggested Lections

Organ

Chr. 29: 25–29; Rev. 14: 1–3; Luke 19: 37–40.

Prayer Desk

Kgs. 8: 27–30 (–53); 1 Pet. 5: 6–11; Luke 11: 1–10.

Lectern

Neh. 8: 2–6; 2 Tim. 3: 14–17; Luke 4: 16–21.

Pulpit

Neh. 8: 1–4a, 5–6; 1 Cor. 13: 1–11; Matt. 13: 18–23.

Alms Dish etc.

Mal. 3: 8, 10; 2 Cor. 8: 1–5; Luke 21: 1–4.

Font

Rom. 6: 3–11; Col. 2: 8–12; Titus 3: 3–7; Matt. 28: 18–20.

Holy Table

Kgs. 8: 6–11; Heb. 9: 11–12, 24; Heb. 10: 19–25; John 17: 14–21.

Suggested Hymns

Organ:	1; 9; 366; 371.
Prayer Desk:	20; 70; 71; 107; 117.
Lectern:	128; 130; 133.
Pulpit:	468; 470; 476; 485.
Alms Dish:	456; 458; 459.
Font:	208; 548; 550.
Holy Table:	307; 564; 565; 575.

DISMISSALS AND BENEDICTIONS*

The grace of the Lord Jesus Christ, and the love of God, and the communion of the Holy Ghost, be with you all.

The grace of the Lord Jesus Christ, and the love of God, and fellowship in the Holy Spirit, be with you all.

The Lord bless you, and keep you: the Lord make his face to shine upon you, and be gracious unto you: the Lord lift up his countenance upon you, and give you peace.

May God himself, the God of peace, make you holy in every part, and keep you sound in spirit, soul, and body, without fault when our Lord Jesus Christ comes.

Now may the God of peace who brought again from the dead our Lord Jesus, the great shepherd of the sheep, by the blood of the eternal covenant, equip you with everything good that you may do his will, working in you that which is pleasing in his sight, through Jesus Christ, to whom be glory for ever and ever.

Grace, mercy and peace from God the Father, Son, and Holy Spirit, be with you and remain with you always.

Go in peace to love and serve the Lord.
And may almighty God bless you, the Father, and the Son, and the Holy Spirit.

*Since it belongs to the office of the ministry "to bless the people from God" the word "you" above should be replaced by "us" when persons not ordained to the ministry are conducting worship.

To God's gracious mercy and protection we comm
you.
And the blessing of God Almighty, the Father, tl
Son, and the Holy Spirit, be amongst you and rema
with you for ever.

Go forth into the world in peace; be of good courag
hold fast that which is good; render to no man e\
for evil; strengthen the fainthearted; support tl
weak; help the afflicted; honour all men; love ar
serve the Lord, rejoicing in the power of the Ho
Spirit. And the blessing of God Almighty, the Fathe
the Son, and the Holy Spirit, be amongst you ar
remain with you always.

The blessing of God, Father, Son, and Holy Spir
descend upon you and on all your work and worsh
in his Name. May he give light to guide you, coura;
to support you and love to unite you, now and alway

May the love of the Lord Jesus draw us to himsel
may the power of the Lord Jesus strengthen us fe
his service; may the joy of the Lord Jesus fill o
souls; and the blessing of God Almighty, Father, So
and Holy Spirit be amongst you and remain with yc
always.